World Holidays

A Watts Guide for Children

Heather Moehn

FRANKLIN WATTS
A Division of Grolier Publishing
New York • London • Hong Kong • Sydney
Danbury, Connecticut

To the Reader

This book contains more than 100 entries chosen to introduce you to the special customs and practices of people around the world. Included here are religious holidays, national celebrations, harvest festivals, and observances tied to natural events such as the beginning of spring. Of course, there are many holidays that could not be included here. In preparing this book, we have tried to include holidays from different parts of the world and different cultures. In reading through the articles, you will see that the many different holidays have a striking number of similarities as well. In every article, you will see other holiday names in small capital letters, LIKE THIS. These are cross-references or "See also" references to related articles in the book. Some words that may be new to you are defined in the Glossary at the back of the book. If you want to learn more about a specific holiday, turn to the Bibliography for a list of other books on world holidays.

Copyright © 2000 by The Rosen Publishing Group, Inc.

Fifth Edition

Library of Congress Cataloging-in-Publication Data

Moehn, Heather.
    World Holidays : a Watts guide for children / Heather Moehn.
      p. cm.
    Includes bibliographical references.
    Summary: An Illustrated alphabetical guide to celebrations and holidays around the world, including religious, civic, and cultural practices.
      ISBN 0-531-11714-6   ISBN 0-531-16490-X (pbk.)
   1. Holidays Juvenile literature. 2. Festivals Juvenile literature. 3. Fasts and feasts Juvenile literature. [1. Festivals. 2. Holidays.] I. Title.
GT3932.M64 2000
394.26—dc21

99-14673
CIP

Manufactured in the United States of America

Published in 2000 by Franklin Watts, a division of Grolier Publishing Co., Inc.

Contents

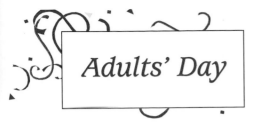

Adults' Day

Adults' Day, also known as Coming of Age Day or Seijin-no-hi, is observed on January 15 in Japan.

Centuries ago, it was one of the most important days in a young person's life. The ceremony for males was called *gempuku,* which literally means "putting on adult clothing." Young men received a new name and adult clothing. The ceremony for young women was called *mogi,* which means "putting on the kimono." After Adults' Day, young people took on adult responsibilities and civic duties.

Today, Adults' Day honors men and women who turned twenty the previous year. At twenty, they are legally adults and have the right to vote, sign contracts, and marry. As symbols of their new status, the young adults receive business suits and formal kimonos. *See* CHILDREN'S DAY.

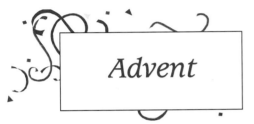

Advent

Advent begins four Sundays before CHRISTMAS and lasts until Christmas Eve. It is celebrated by many Christians around the world.

The name *Advent* is from a Latin word meaning "coming" or "arrival." During Advent, Christians prepare to celebrate the arrival of Jesus on Christmas, the day of his birth.

Children count the days until Christmas on an Advent calendar, which is sometimes designed like a house with shuttered windows. Each day, the child opens a shutter to reveal a Christmas scene or symbol. On Christmas Eve, the last window is uncovered, showing the Nativity scene with Mary, Joseph, and the infant Jesus.

Advent wreaths are displayed in homes and churches. They are made of evergreen branches around which four candles are placed. Each week, the family lights one candle so that all four glow on Christmas Day. *See* EASTER *and* EPIPHANY.

Advent calendars come in many shapes. On this Advent calendar, each day is represented by a numbered stocking. A child pulls something out of a different stocking each day.

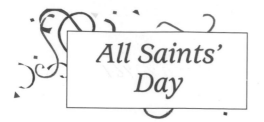

All Saints' Day

All Saints' Day is observed on November 1 by Roman Catholics, Anglicans, and Orthodox Christians around the world. Also known as All Hallow's Day or All-Hallomas, it is a day that honors all the Christian saints and martyrs, especially those who do not have feast days of their own. Greek Christians first celebrated this holiday in the fourth century. It was not established as an official holiday until the seventh century, when Pope Boniface IV dedicated the Pantheon in Rome to the Virgin Mary and all the saints.

All Saints' Day is a happy holiday with music and rejoicing in the churches. People celebrate the goodness of the saints and remember the martyrs who gave their lives for their faith. On the next day, ALL SOULS' DAY, the mood turns somber, as people pray for the souls of their deceased family members and friends. *See* EID AL-ADHA.

All Souls' Day

Roman Catholics, Anglicans, and Orthodox Christians around the world celebrate All Souls' Day on November 2. They honor the souls of the recently deceased, who are waiting in purgatory to enter heaven. The date follows ALL SAINTS' DAY, which commemorates the holy men and women already in heaven.

During the Middle Ages, adults went "souling" in the British Isles. On All Souls' Eve, November 1, people walked from door to door offering prayers for the dead and receiving soul cakes in return. According to legend, whenever a soul cake was eaten, it helped release a soul from purgatory into heaven. Soul cakes are still popular in Great Britain, Belgium, southern Germany, and Austria.

On All Souls' Day, church services are held, and prayers are said for the dead. Graves are cleaned and adorned with flowers, crosses, wreaths, and other decorations. Candles and lanterns are often left burning all night to help brighten the darkness for the souls. In Europe, picnics are held in cemeteries, and any food that is not eaten is left for the departed. *See* DAY OF THE DEAD *and* OBON.

People light candles, pray, and offer gifts of flowers and crosses to shorten the souls' time in purgatory before they are accepted into heaven.

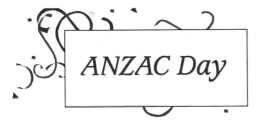

ANZAC Day

ANZAC Day is celebrated on April 25 in Australia and New Zealand. ANZAC stands for Australian and New Zealand Army Corps. This holiday honors the bravery of the ANZAC troops who served in World War I.

On April 25, 1915, ANZAC troops stormed the Gallipoli Peninsula near Istanbul, Turkey. After fighting five Turkish divisions and suffering more than 8,000 dead and 19,000 wounded,

The heroic soldiers of the ANZAC forces are celebrated with parades and ceremonies.

the troops secured an area that became known as Anzac Cove. The survivors were heartbroken when they were ordered to evacuate the cove later in the year.

ANZAC Day was set aside in the early 1920s to honor the troops who fought in World War I. As Australian and New Zealand troops fought in other wars, the holiday expanded to honor veterans of World War II, the Korean War, the Vietnam War, and the Gulf War. The day is celebrated with church services, parades, and ceremonies at war memorials. *See* MEMORIAL DAY, PULASKI DAY, *and* VETERANS' DAY.

April Fools' Day

April Fools' Day is celebrated on April 1 in England, Scotland, France, and the United States. It is a day spent tricking friends and playing practical jokes.

It is believed by some that the tradition began in France in the 1500s. According to calendars used at that time, April 1 was New Year's Day. In 1582, Pope Gregory XIII introduced a new calendar that changed New Year's Day to January 1. Because of poor communication, many people didn't hear about the change right away. They continued to celebrate on April 1 and became known as April fools. This led to the custom of fooling people, a custom that soon spread to other countries. Many names for the fool are used around the world. In England the person tricked is a noddie or gawby. In Scotland the fool is a gowk or a cuckoo. In France people try to pin paper fish on other people's backs without getting caught. The person wearing the fish is called a *poisson d'avril,* or "April fish." *See* LEAP YEAR DAY.

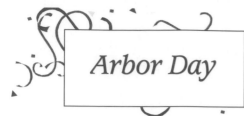

Arbor Day

Arbor Day is officially celebrated on the last Friday in April in the United States. But since planting times vary around the country, each state has its own day of celebration.

People plant as many trees as possible on Arbor Day.

The word *arbor* is Latin, and it means "tree." Arbor Day was created when a settler named J. Sterling Morton moved to the Nebraska Territory, a treeless plain. Morton missed trees and realized how important they were for keeping the soil in place, giving shade, and providing fuel and lumber. He decided that a special day should be set aside for trees and offered prizes to people who planted the most. Everyone liked the idea, and on April 10, 1872, more than one million trees were planted.

Arbor Day celebrations can be found all around the country. Each year the president and the first lady plant a tree on the grounds of the White House. People plant trees along highways and in parks and playgrounds. *See* EARTH DAY *and* TU BI-SHEVAT.

Arbor Day Across America

National Arbor Day is the last Friday in April, but many states observe Arbor Day according to their best tree-planting times. Check the list below to find out when Arbor Day is observed near you.

Alabama—Last full week in February
Alaska—Third Monday in May
Arizona—Last Friday in April
Arkansas—Third Monday in March
California—March 7–14
Colorado—Third Friday in April
Connecticut—April 30
Delaware—Last Friday in April
District of Columbia—Last Friday in April
Florida—Third Friday in January
Georgia—Third Friday in February
Hawaii—First Friday in November
Idaho—Last Friday in April
Illinois—Last Friday in April
Indiana—Last Friday in April
Iowa—Last Friday in April
Kansas—Last Friday in March
Kentucky—First Friday in April

Louisiana—Third Friday in January
Maine—Third full week in May
Maryland—First Wednesday in April
Massachusetts—April 28–May 5
Michigan—Last Friday in April
Minnesota—Last Friday in April
Mississippi—Second Friday in February
Missouri—First Friday in April
Montana—Last Friday in April
Nebraska—Last Friday in April
Nevada—Last Friday in April
New Hampshire—Last Friday in April
New Jersey—Last Friday in April
New Mexico—Second Friday in March
New York—Last Friday in April
North Carolina—First Friday after March 15
North Dakota—First Friday in May

Ohio—Last Friday in April
Oklahoma—Last Full week in March
Oregon—First full week in April
Pennsylvania—Last Friday in April
Rhode Island—Last Friday in April
South Carolina—First Friday in December
South Dakota—Last Friday in April
Tennessee—First Friday in March
Texas—Last Friday in April
Utah—Last Friday in April
Vermont—First Friday in May
Virginia—Second Friday in April
Washington—Second Wednesday in April
West Virginia—Second Friday in April
Wisconsin—Last Friday in April
Wyoming—Last Monday in April

Ash Wednesday

Ash Wednesday occurs forty days before EASTER and marks the first day of LENT. It is observed by Roman Catholics, Anglicans, and Orthodox Christians around the world.

Ash Wednesday gets its name from a custom started by Pope Gregory I in the sixth century. Priests make the sign of the cross on the foreheads of the devout with ashes, a symbol of repentance and a reminder of the shortness of human life. As the priest marks each person's forehead, he says, "Remember that you are dust, and unto dust you shall return."

In Spain it is a custom to bury a thin strip of meat on Ash Wednesday, symbolizing the burial of worldly possessions and the abstinence from eating meat during Lent. In Iceland, children try to stick bags of ashes on people's backs without getting caught. *See* RAMADAN *and* ROSH HASHANAH.

A priest uses the ashes of palms burned on PALM SUNDAY of the previous year to mark worshipers' foreheads.

Ashura

Ashura is an Islamic holy day celebrated on the tenth of Muharram, the first month of the Islamic year. It is observed in India, Iraq, and Turkey and by Shi'ite Muslims throughout Asia.

Ashura commemorates the death of Husain, the grandson of the prophet Muhammad, in A.D. 680. While traveling to present-day Iraq, Husain and his Shi'ite followers were surrounded by Sunnis. Shi'ites and Sunnis are separate branches of the Islamic faith. Like many religious opponents, they have often fought each other. The Sunnis prevented the Shi'ites from drinking water from the nearby Euphrates River. Husain, weakened by thirst, died in battle. His body was buried in Kaerbala, a small town on the banks of the Euphrates that is now considered a sacred place by Shi'ite Muslims.

Ashura was established by Muhammad as a voluntary day on which to fast and atone. On this day, people wear mourning clothes and do not bathe or shave. They eat a special sherbet in honor of the thirst felt by Husain. Black tents are set up in the streets, and the story of Husain's suffering is told. People also perform a play called *ta'ziyah,* which depicts the death of Husain and the struggle of the Shi'ites. *See* JOAN OF ARC, FEAST OF, *and* ST. JOSEPH'S DAY.

5

Assumption Day

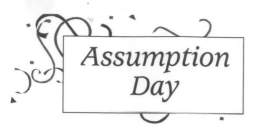

Assumption Day is observed on August 15 by Roman Catholics, Anglicans, and Orthodox Christians around the world. It is usually regarded as the principal feast day of the Virgin Mary, the mother of Jesus.

When Mary died, the apostle Thomas missed her funeral. He was so sad that he asked to have her tomb opened so that he could see her one last time. When he looked inside, however, the tomb was empty. It became an official belief of the church that Mary's body did not remain on Earth but was assumed, or taken, into heaven to be reunited with her soul.

In some parts of Europe, the day is known as the Feast of Our Lady of the Harvest. In Armenia, people are not permitted to eat grapes from the new harvest until Assumption Day. Then a tray of grapes is blessed at the church, and everyone is able to enjoy them. In southern Brazil, the feast is called Our Lady of the Navigators. People decorate canoes, play music, and travel to other villages to entertain and feast. *See* EASTER *and* KWANZAA.

Ati-Atihan Festival

The Ati-Atihan Festival is celebrated in the Philippines on the third weekend in January.

Ati-Atihan means "to cause to be like the Ati." The Ati were small, dark people who lived on the Philippine island of Panay centuries ago. Legend says that they gave land to people who were forced to flee their homeland of Borneo. In gratitude, the new arrivals darkened their faces to look like the Ati. Years later, Spanish missionaries settled in the area and converted many of the people to Christianity. However, they feared the spread of Islamic religions by Muslims who were moving into the area. The Spanish persuaded the natives to darken their faces and wear war costumes to frighten away the Muslims. The plan worked.

Today the Ati-Atihan Festival is a colorful and frenzied celebration. People cover their faces with soot and wear fancy costumes of feathers, shells, and leaves. Drums beat as people dance the same rhythmic steps over and over while shouting, *"Hala bira!"* meaning "Go and fight!" *See* WAITANGI DAY.

Hundreds of people celebrate the Ati-Atihan Festival in Visayan Islands, the Philippines.

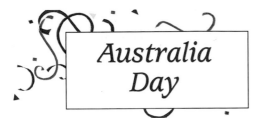

Australia Day

Australia Day, formerly called Foundation Day or Anniversary Day, is celebrated on January 26. The day commemorates the founding of the first British settlement in Australia.

In 1788, Captain Arthur Philip landed at Botany Bay on the southeastern coast of Australia. His fleet carried 1,500 people, nearly 800 of whom were convicts. In

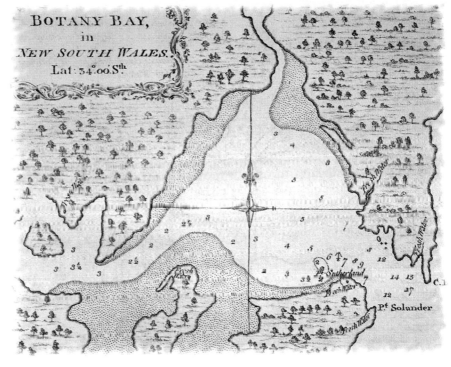

Botany Bay was named for the many unusual plants that grew on its shores when Captain Arthur Philip landed there in 1788.

England at the time, people were put in prison for debt and other minor crimes. Because of the harsh sentences, prisons were overcrowded. England's solution was to ship convicts to colonies overseas.

Captain Philip moved from Botany Bay to Port Jackson, and on January 26 he raised the British flag over the area, which grew to become Sydney, Australia's largest city.

Australia Day was first celebrated in Sydney in 1817. On that day, at Botany Bay, the first landing is reenacted. A flag-raising ceremony is held in Sydney, and descendants of the first immigrants dress in eighteenth-century costumes. Cities throughout the country hold carnivals, special art exhibits, and fireworks displays. *See* BERCHTOLD'S DAY.

Baby's First Haircut

Among Native Americans in Peru and Bolivia, it is customary to let a baby's hair grow for the first few years of its life. The first haircut is considered a special occasion. The baby sits in a high chair with everyone gathered around. The hair is combed and separated into locks tied with brightly colored ribbons, one lock for each guest. The godfather cuts the first lock and presents his gift, usually land, money, or an animal. Then the guests cut the remaining locks and give their presents. The money is saved for when the child is older. *See* TOL.

Bastille Day

Bastille Day is celebrated on July 14 in France, New Caledonia, Tahiti, and other French territories. It is known as the birthday of the French Republic.

In the eighteenth century, France was ruled by King Louis XVI and his queen, Marie Antoinette. The powerful king was often cruel, and the people could do little to stop him.

The economy was poor under their rule. Many people starved in winter, whereas aristocrats always had enough to eat. This angered people, and they began to resent the king, who showed no concern for their problems. When told that the people had little food and no bread to eat, Marie Antoinette mocked their misery by saying, "Let them eat cake."

The king and queen imprisoned people who opposed them in the Bastille, a huge prison with 100-foot-high stone walls and eight towers. Prisoners included many famous writers, philosophers, and political activists.

At the same time, many new ideas about the rights of the people, freedom, liberty, and justice were spreading across Europe and North America. In France, university students and workers met secretly to discuss how the people could win these basic rights.

On July 14, 1789, a young revolutionary leader named Camille Desmoulins led the people into action. They stormed the Bastille, released all the prisoners, and took the ammunition. This dramatic action is considered the start of the French Revolution.

Like the Revolutionary War in the United States, the French Revolution led to a complete change in the ways of governing. The king's total power was

In Paris, the Eiffel Tower is lit by a fireworks display during celebrations on Bastille Day.

8

destroyed, and the people were given a role in ruling themselves. Under the new system, all people were considered equal.

Bastille Day was declared a French national holiday in 1880. Each year, celebrations are held in many French cities and towns. In Paris the day begins with a 100-cannon salute. Then a grand parade goes down the main street, Champs-Élysées. All day there is music and dancing in different parts of the city. The blue, white, and red colors of the French flag can be seen everywhere. At night, the festivities continue as loud and colorful fireworks explode in the sky.

In Tahiti and the rest of French Polynesia, the celebration lasts almost the entire

The Bastille Day parade may include marching bands, dancers, and people wearing costumes reflecting the period of the revolution.

month of July. The festivities include many unique Polynesian activities. Competitions are a big part of the celebration. People try their luck and skill at canoe races, javelin-throwing contests, and foot races while carrying baskets of fruit. The highlight of the celebration is the folklore spectacle seen every night of the month. Groups from all over French Polynesia give amazing music and dance performances.

Throughout these celebrations, French people remember that they are celebrating the freedom, liberty, and equality that was won for them many years ago. *See* CINCO DE MAYO, INDEPENDENCE DAY, *and* POLISH CONSTITUTION DAY.

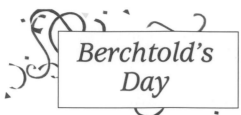

Berchtold's Day

Berchtold's Day is celebrated on January 2 in Switzerland. It honors Duke Berchtold V, who founded the capital city of Bern in the twelfth century.

Legend says that the duke built the city to show his gratitude to heaven after he survived a bear attack while hunting. The name Bern comes from the German word for "bear," *baren*. The bear is the emblem of the city and can be seen on signs, sculptures, and paintings throughout Bern.

Berchtold's Day is a favorite holiday with children. Neighborhoods hold parties where the kids sing, dance, eat, and play games. Children play a traditional game in which four nuts are placed in a square and a fifth nut is placed on top. Since the ground is usually covered by snow in January, children begin collecting nuts for Berchtold's Day in early autumn. *See* AUSTRALIA DAY.

Boxing Day

Boxing Day is held on December 26 in Great Britain, Canada, and Australia. In South Africa, a similar holiday is known as Day of Good Will.

The custom of Boxing Day began during medieval times. During the year, servants and tradespeople carried little boxes in which they collected tips and gifts. They traditionally waited until the day after CHRISTMAS to open the boxes, since Christmas was when the most money was given. The method of collecting gifts was called "boxing," the gifts were "boxes," and the day became known as Boxing Day.

Boxing Day has traditionally been the time to give tips to service providers such as mail carriers, garbage collectors, hairdressers, and waitresses. At one time, ministers were expected to provide bread, cheese, and beer for their parishioners. In recent years, the custom of Boxing Day has faded as fewer people carry boxes, and gifts are generally given on or before Christmas. However, most people still remember the spirit of the holiday by saying thanks and giving large tips on the day. *See* EID AL-FITR.

This picture shows a child giving a present to a country postal worker, as is customary on Boxing Day.

Canada Day

Canada Day, formerly known as Dominion Day, is celebrated in Canada on July 1.

Canada was a British colony, like the thirteen American colonies. But Canada did not declare its independence. As increasing numbers of British colonists settled in Canada during the nineteenth century, they became unhappy about their relationship with Great Britain. They believed that they were not represented fairly in legislative assemblies and that British leaders were too far away to make good decisions. Britain tried to appease them by combining Upper and Lower Canada (present-day Ontario and Quebec) into one colony called the Province of Canada and giving the people limited power to rule themselves. But the colonists continued to fight for their freedom.

On July 1, 1867, the British Parliament passed the British North America Act (BNA), which united the Province of Canada and the colonies of Nova Scotia and New Brunswick into a new nation called the Dominion of Canada. As a dominion, Canada was able to rule itself, but its government had to be based on the British system. The Dominion slowly gained more freedom, and the British Parliament officially recognized Canada as an independent nation in 1931.

On Canada Day, people remember the signing of the BNA and the birthday of Canada. The name of the holiday was changed from Dominion Day to Canada Day in 1982 to symbolize the complete break from colonial rule. Canadians celebrate the day much the way Americans celebrate INDEPENDENCE DAY. Cities hold parades and fairs. Bands play, the Canadian flag waves, and people picnic with friends and family. At night the festivities continue with dancing and fireworks. *See* CENTRAL AFRICAN REPUBLIC INDEPENDENCE DAY.

Royal Guards, reminders of historic ties to Britain, march past Parliament Hill in Ottawa on Canada Day.

Central African Republic Independence Day

Central African Republic Independence Day is celebrated on August 13. It commemorates the establishment of an independent nation in 1960.

In the 1880s, France claimed a large section of central Africa. The Europeans who settled there exploited the land's resources of diamonds and gold. They abused their power and treated the native Africans very poorly. The African people protested against these conditions. The most violent revolts occurred between 1928 and 1930. In 1946, France gave the colony its own legislature. It was represented in the French National Assembly by Barthélemy Boganda. Mr. Boganda led a powerful movement for independence. In 1958 the colony gained autonomy and became known as the Central African Republic. Two years later, on August 13, 1960, the Central African Republic became fully independent.

People celebrate the day with parades. They perform traditional music and dances. Families gather to cook and share elaborate meals. *See* BASTILLE DAY, CANADA DAY, *and* JAMHURI DAY.

People play traditional music at public celebrations on Central African Republic Independence Day. Here, Gbayan men perform music using the kinds of large drums that have been used for many generations.

Children's Day

Children's Day, Kodomo-no-hi, is celebrated on May 5 in Japan and in Japanese communities around the world.

When Children's Day originated hundreds of years ago, it honored boys. A separate holiday, the DOLL FESTIVAL, was held for girls. In 1948, Children's Day became a holiday for both boys and girls. However, some special customs still make the two holidays different.

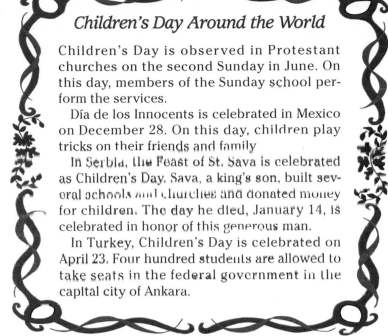

Children's Day Around the World

Children's Day is observed in Protestant churches on the second Sunday in June. On this day, members of the Sunday school perform the services.

Día de los Innocents is celebrated in Mexico on December 28. On this day, children play tricks on their friends and family.

In Serbia, the Feast of St. Sava is celebrated as Children's Day. Sava, a king's son, built several schools and churches and donated money for children. The day he died, January 14, is celebrated in honor of this generous man.

In Turkey, Children's Day is celebrated on April 23. Four hundred students are allowed to take seats in the federal government in the capital city of Ankara.

At the beginning of the festival, families fly streamers decorated like carp from poles outside their homes. They consider carp the fish of success, possessing strength, courage, and determination. Parents hope that their children will have qualities like the carp.

Families display samurai warrior dolls, helmets, suits of armor, and swords for boys. The girls' dolls are saved for the Doll Festival. Children's Day is a popular time for karate, judo, and kendo contests.

Children's Day is a time of fun for kids, with singing, dancing, puppet shows, and plays about favorite legends. Children also make crafts. They create their own carp streamers and attach them to sticks to make them swim through the air. They also make beautiful kites. Instructors show them how to do origami, the art of folding paper into shapes. They create birds, boats, and flowers out of one square sheet without cutting or pasting. All the children's favorite foods are prepared on Children's Day. *See* ADULTS' DAY *and* RAKSHA BANDHAMA.

On Children's Day, boys and girls dress in traditional Japanese clothing. This young girl is wearing a kimono, *a garment that was first worn in the fifth century. It is held together by a wide belt, called an* obi.

13

Chinese New Year

The Chinese New Year starts on the first day of the new lunar cycle (between January 20 and February 20) and lasts for fifteen days. It is celebrated in China and by Chinese communities all over the world.

The New Year is the most important Chinese festival. Legend says that the holiday began when a wild beast called a *nian* appeared at the end of winter to attack villagers. (In Chinese, *nian* also means "year.") At first, people were afraid of this creature, but they discovered that it feared three things: bright lights, the color red, and noise. So they built a huge bonfire, set off firecrackers, and painted their doors red. The *nian* covered its head and fled. Those three elements play an important role in the New Year celebration.

The festivities begin on the last night of the old year. One ceremony honors the Kitchen God, who is believed to watch the family's actions all year. On New Year's Eve he leaves Earth and gives his report to the Jade Emperor in heaven. To help him on his journey, families provide a farewell dinner and make offerings of sweet cakes and preserved fruits. They also dip his picture in wine and smear his lips with honey so that he will be in a sweet mood when he gives his report.

On New Year's Eve, Chinese people seal the doors of their homes with strips of red paper to keep out bad spirits. They decorate the doors with "lucky phrases" written in gold ink, meant to bring good fortune and prosperity. This popular tradition is more than a thousand years old.

The Chinese Calendar Year

The Chinese year is based on the cycles of the moon. Each year consists of about twelve months. Each month begins with the new moon (when the moon is not visible in the sky) and has twenty-nine or thirty days. A month is repeated seven times during each nineteen-year period. This keeps the calendar in line with the seasons. The year starts with the second new moon after the beginning of winter. Chinese New Year never occurs earlier than January 20 or later than February 20.

In addition to parades and dances, people go to street fairs held during the Chinese New Year.

On New Year's Day, the seals are broken, and the doors are opened to let in good luck. Scissors and knives are not used because they might cut the good fortune. Brooms are not used either for fear that they will sweep out the luck. All debts have been paid and all quarrels settled, so everyone can start the New Year with a clean slate.

During the two-week celebration, China is abloom with flowers. So is New York City's Chinatown, San Francisco's Chinatown, and other areas around the world in which there is a large Chinese population. Each flower has a special meaning. The blossoms of peach and plum trees signify long life, the white narcissus brings good fortune, and the camellia symbolizes springtime.

Acrobats, jugglers, clowns, and musicians perform in the streets. One popular performance is the Dragon Dance. The dragon is made out of paper or silk stretched over bamboo poles. It can be as long as fifty feet. A dozen people carry it. They make the dragon twist and dance through the streets, chasing a yellow globe that represents the sun. Legend says that if the dragon catches the globe, the sun will go out. The dragon never catches it, and the performance ends with a burst of fireworks.

Finally, on the fifteenth day of the holiday, the full moon rises. This is the last day of the New Year's festival and is celebrated with the Lantern Festival. Thousands of lanterns hang in the streets, making the night sky look as bright as day. They all have a special shape: there are birds, fish, stars, and flowers made from paper, glass, or silk. *See* KOREAN NEW YEAR, NEW YEAR'S DAY, *and* VIETNAMESE NEW YEAR.

This dragon will crouch, spin, jump, leap, and run as people inside the costume perform the Dragon Dance.

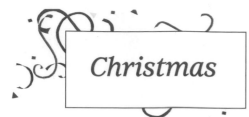

Christmas is celebrated by Christians throughout the world on December 25. It is one of the most important and most joyous holidays of the year for Christians because it celebrates the birth of Jesus, their messiah.

Before Jesus was born, his parents, Mary and Joseph, traveled to Bethlehem to pay taxes and be counted in a census. On the night Mary knew that she was going to give birth, they went searching for shelter. All the inns were full. Finally an innkeeper allowed the couple to stay in his barn. Jesus was born that night among farm animals. Angels told shepherds of his birth, and they immediately visited the infant Jesus. A star appeared above the stable, leading three Wise Men to the place. They came bearing gifts of gold, frankincense, and myrrh.

Each year, the story of the birth of Jesus is told. Many schools and churches hold pageants acting out the tale. Nativity scenes, or crèches, with figures representing the birth of Jesus are displayed. In Italy the scene is called *presepio*. This custom is believed to have started with St. Francis of Assisi in 1223. He used real people and live animals to tell the story.

Christmas began as a religious holiday, but during the Middle Ages, it became a day for having fun. Today people celebrate Christmas for both religious and fun-filled reasons.

One favorite belief about Christmas is Santa Claus. Legend says that on Christmas Eve, this jolly fellow brings gifts to children who have been good all year. People believe that Santa is modeled after St. Nicholas, a fourth-century bishop. He gave gifts to children when they behaved and disciplined them if they were bad. He was said to have heard about a man who was so poor he was going to sell his daughters into slavery.

New Holiday

Christmas replaced the pagan holiday Saturnalia, which was held on the day of the winter solstice, December 22. Saturnalia was dedicated to the renewed power of the sun and to the god of agriculture.

The three Wise Men offer their gifts to the infant Jesus as Mary and Joseph look on. In southern France, small Nativity scenes with santons (little saints) are put up. In Italy, Nativity scenes called presepios can be found in homes and churches.

St. Nicholas saved the family by throwing sacks of gold down the chimney of the man's house. One sack fell into a stocking that was hanging by the fireplace to dry. Since then, children have hung stockings in the hope that Santa will leave them a gift.

People also give each other gifts on Christmas. Some believe that the

Decorating Christmas trees is a 500-year-old tradition.

custom started with the gifts the Wise Men brought to the infant Jesus. In Russia, the grandmother, or *babushka*, brings the gifts. Legend says that she is an old woman who deliberately gave the Wise Men wrong directions on their journey to visit Jesus. She later regretted her behavior. To make up for it, she gives gifts on Christmas Day.

In many countries, families decorate a Christmas tree in their homes with lights, ornaments, tinsel, and a star or angel on the top. The first Christmas trees could be found in Germany in the 1500s. At that time, German families built a *Weihnachtspyramide*—a wooden pyramid covered with evergreen branches. Some historians believe that this was related to the "Paradise tree" featured in medieval plays. A Paradise tree was a fir tree decorated with apples and surrounded by candles. It symbolized a legend involving the biblical figures Adam and Eve. According to the legend, when Adam left Paradise, he took with him a seed from the Tree of Knowledge. A tree grew from the seed, and wood from that tree was used for the cross on which Jesus was crucified.

Carols are another popular way to celebrate Christmas. The earliest Christmas carol in English is from around 1410. Some carols focus on the religious aspects of Christmas; others are just for fun. Groups of people walk from house to house singing carols. Often they receive a warm drink and cookies. In Romania, children go caroling with a large wooden star on top of a stick called a *steaua*. It is covered with paper and ribbons, and in the center is a picture of the holy family lit by a candle.

Christmas is a time when families and friends gather. It is also a time to remember the less fortunate. Many people donate toys and food to shelters. Classrooms often "adopt" a needy family and raise money to help them during the holidays. Children visit hospitals and nursing homes and sing carols. *See* CONFUCIUS'S BIRTHDAY, KWANZAA, *and* MUHAMMAD'S BIRTHDAY.

Cinco de Mayo

Cinco de Mayo, which means the fifth of May, is celebrated on that day in Mexico and by Mexican American communities in the United States.

In 1861 the ruler of France, Napoleon III, wanted to make Mexico a French colony. France had lent Mexico money during the Mexican American War of 1846–1848, and Napoleon III decided that the Mexican leaders were not repaying the debt fast enough. He thought that taking over Mexico would be easy.

French troops landed in Veracruz, the largest port city, and began to march toward Mexico City. Along the way, they camped near a small town called Puebla. The Mexican general Ignacio Zaragoza and 5,000 mestizos and Zapotec Indians were waiting for them. Zaragoza hoped to stall the French long enough for the people in Mexico City to prepare for battle.

On May 5, 1861, Zaragoza placed his men on the tops of two hills. When the French ran up the hills, the Mexican troops fired muskets and cannons, forcing most of the French troops back. However, the Mexicans had very little ammunition, so that strategy could not work for long. Luckily it began to rain. The hills became so muddy and slippery that the French could not advance. After four hours of trying to fight, they gave up and retreated. The small and untrained Mexican army had defeated the French!

The French quickly regrouped and were able to take over Mexico City. But the victory at Puebla gave the Mexican people the courage to keep fighting. Finally on April 2, 1867, they succeeded in defeating the French and forcing them out of the country.

The Mexican coat of arms is based on a legend that says the Aztecs built Tenochtitlán, now Mexico City, where they saw an eagle devouring a snake on top of a cactus. The coat of arms is centered on the flag.

18

In addition to feasts, fireworks, and games, dancing is a common part of Cinco de Mayo. Some of the dances, such as the flamenco, above, originated from the culture of Andalusian Gypsies.

Each year, Mexicans celebrate the victory of the Battle of Puebla. They take pride in the strength and perseverance that their ancestors displayed in battle. Street fairs, usually including parades, patriotic speeches, and folk dancing, are held in most cities. Mariachi bands play Mexican folk songs. The musicians wear colorful costumes as they play violins, guitars, trumpets, and basses. Traditional Mexican food is served, such as enchiladas (a rolled-up tortilla filled with chopped meat, chicken, or cheese), frijoles (beans), and tamales (cornmeal steamed in corn husks and mixed with pork or chicken). A favorite treat is *churros*, long pieces of fried dough covered with sugar. Children take turns hitting a piñata with a stick while blindfolded. The piñata is a papier-mâché figure filled with candy. When it breaks open, everyone scrambles to collect the candy that falls to the ground. *See* MEMORIAL DAY *and* ANZAC DAY.

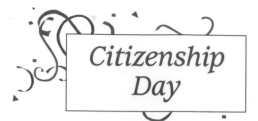

Citizenship Day

Citizenship Day is observed on September 17 in the United States. Congress created the holiday in 1952, replacing Constitution Day and I Am American Day, to commemorate the signing of the U.S. Constitution and celebrate the rights of citizenship. September 17 was chosen because it was on that day in 1787 that the Constitution was signed at Independence Hall in Philadelphia. The Constitution created a federal government that enabled the United States to grow and expand.

Citizenship Day honors all the citizens of the United States, those who were born U.S. citizens and those who have been naturalized. A person who is naturalized has come from another country and chosen to become a U.S. citizen. Citizenship Day is a day to reflect on and appreciate the rights and freedoms that are guaranteed by the Constitution. *See* POLISH CONSTITUTION DAY.

Columbus Day

Columbus Day is October 12, but it is observed on the second Monday in October in the United States. Christopher Columbus was an Italian explorer and navigator. In 1492 he convinced the king and queen of Spain to fund an expedition to find a shorter trade route to Asia. Convinced that the world was round, Columbus was going to sail west to reach the Far East.

Columbus set sail with three ships, the *Niña*, the *Pinta*, and the *Santa Maria*, on August 3, 1492. On October 12, he and his crew saw land and thought that they had made it to Asia. However, they had actually landed in America. Columbus's arrival in the New World introduced Europeans to new cultures and new plants, animals, and foods . Millions of Native Americans died as a result of diseases brought by the Europeans and because of wars fought over land. When people celebrate Columbus's success, they should also remember the terrible effects it had on the Native Americans.

Across the United States, people celebrate the day Columbus landed in America because it changed the course of history. On Columbus Day, businesses are closed, and cities have parades with floats and bands. Special ceremonies are held at monuments honoring Columbus. *See* AUSTRALIA DAY.

Columbus was the first person to explore the Western world for the Spanish Empire, but he was not the first European to land there. The Vikings had landed in North America nearly five hundred years earlier.

Confucius's Birthday

Confucius's Birthday is celebrated on September 28 in China and by followers of Confucianism around the world.

Confucius was born in 551 B.C. He traveled all over China teaching philosophy and ethics. He believed that people should possess five virtues to be moral: kindness, uprightness, decorum, wisdom, and faithfulness. His Golden Rule was "Do unto others as you would have others do unto you."

During his lifetime, the government of China was corrupt. Confucius held several political offices in his home state of Lu. He put his teachings into practice and was a successful leader. Crime was eliminated, and many reforms were introduced. He was so successful that other leaders feared his power and removed him from office. He spent the rest of his life teaching his views on the classics.

Confucius did not leave a book of writings. Instead his teachings and sayings were learned and passed down by his disciples in a book called The Analects.

Confucianism became a major philosophy in China and is known around the world. His ethical ideals formed the basis for Chinese society. In Ch'ü-fu, his birthplace, a two-week festival is held in honor of his birthday. Ceremonies are performed with traditional music and dance. There are exhibits and lectures on the life and teachings of Confucius. *See* CHRISTMAS, MUHAMMAD'S BIRTHDAY, *and* MORMON PIONEER DAY.

Feast of Corpus Christi

The Feast of Corpus Christi is held on the Thursday sixty days after EASTER. It is observed by Catholics around the world.

Legend says that the holy day began after a nun named Juliana saw a vision in which part of the moon had been broken away. God told her that the moon represented the church and that the break showed the people's lack of respect for the Eucharist. The Eucharist is a Christian sacrament commemorating the Last Supper. Bread and wine are blessed and become the body and blood of Jesus Christ. (Corpus Christi means "body of Christ.") After Juliana's vision, people began holding the Corpus Christi festival in honor of the sacrament. They carried the bread and wine in a procession through town after Mass.

In Spain, Italy, France, and Portugal, the grand procession is still held. In some places, people carry the bread and wine over a bed of rose petals. Houses along the route are decorated with flowers, crosses, and pictures of Christ. In the United States, a ceremony is performed in which the sacrament is blessed and hymns are sung. *See* OUR LADY OF FATIMA DAY.

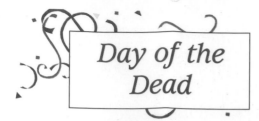

Day of the Dead

The Day of the Dead is celebrated on November 1 and 2 in Mexico and in Mexican communities around the world.

The origins of the holiday can be traced to the Aztecs, who lived in Mexico centuries ago. The Aztecs believed that the souls of the dead were links between the living and the gods. Because of that important role, festivals developed that honored the souls. The Day of the Dead is celebrated as a time when the souls return to their homes to check that everything is going well and to make sure that they have not been forgotten. In parts of Mexico, monarch butterflies migrate to the area during the Day of the Dead celebrations. Since ancient times, it has been believed that the beautiful butterflies carry the spirits of the dead.

To prepare for the Day of the Dead, families create *ofrendas,* or altars, in their homes to welcome back the souls of their departed family and friends. The *ofrendas* are adorned with flowers, candles, and colorful pictures. Incense is burned. This special incense is made from sage and copal, a sap from trees that grow in Mexico. *Ofrendas* usually include items that are familiar to the dead person, such as photographs, articles of clothing, or favorite keepsakes. Good meals are prepared: platters of rice, beans, chicken or red meat in mole sauce, sweet potatoes, and *pan de muerto*—a special sweetbread that is shaped into figures called *animas,* or "souls." Sometimes it is shaped like a dog because it is believed that dogs ferry the souls of the departed across a river into heaven. A washbasin and towel are also provided so that the soul can freshen up before the meal.

The main part of the holiday is the trip to the cemetery. Families carefully tend the graves. Weeds are pulled, and the ground is raked. If there are buildings or crypts for the

In addition to making small statues of the dead and offering food to the dead, people decorate grave sites.

tombs, they are swept and washed. People decorate the graves with flowers, wreaths, and ribbons. They place candles nearby to help light the way for the souls. People also often bring picnics and leave part of the food behind as an offering. Sometimes a mariachi band plays traditional music as people sing along. Outside

On this altar, a family has left offerings of candy skulls, fruits, and a special bread called pan de muerto.

the cemetery gates, vendors sell food and drinks. The mood is festive and joyful as people celebrate the memory of their deceased friends and relatives.

In Mexican American communities in the United States where it is not possible to visit family cemeteries, people hold a special ceremony. They pay tribute to the four directions, each of which represents a group of people who have died. The north honors the elderly and all ancestors; the west honors women; the south honors infants and children; and the east honors men. As people remember family members and friends who have died, they say their names, rattle instruments, and place a marigold blossom in a wreath. Marigolds play a special role in Day of the Dead celebrations. In Mexico people drop marigold petals along the route from the cemeteries to their homes. The flowers' strong scent is believed to help the spirits find their way home.

Day of the Dead celebrations are joyful. While respecting the souls of the dead, the festivities often mock death itself. People wear skeleton costumes and masks. Children run through the streets shouting, *"Calaveras! Calaveras!"* which means "Skulls! Skulls!" People give them candy, fruit, and money. Children also enjoy special candy available only on the Day of the Dead, such as chocolate skulls and sugar coffins. At night, fireworks explode in the sky. Bands play on street corners while people dance and sing. *See* ALL SAINTS' DAY, ALL SOULS' DAY, *and* OBON.

23

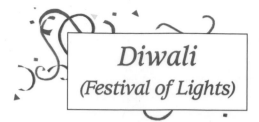
Diwali, or the Festival of Lights, is the most widely observed Hindu festival. It is celebrated during the last two days of the Hindu lunar month Asvina and the first two days of Kartika (September–October). Hindus all around the world celebrate, especially those in India, Malaysia, Mauritius, and Nepal.

The name Diwali comes from a Sanskrit word meaning "row of lights." During the holiday, lamps line the roofs of buildings and windowsills, and streets are filled with strings of lights. People use electric lights, candles, and *dipas*, traditional earthen lamps filled with oil. There are several legends about why so many lights shine during this holiday.

Hindus honor Lakshmi, the goddess of wealth. They believe that during this time she returns from her country home and uses the lamps to help guide her way. People wish for Lakshmi to bring them good fortune and believe she will not bless a house that is not lit up. Elaborate good-luck designs welcome her. They are made out of dyed rice flour and decorate the floors of homes.

Diwali also commemorates the time when the god Rama killed the evil demon Ravana. The entire countryside is lit with thousands of lights to symbolize the victory of good over evil.

Diwali is as important to Hindus as CHRISTMAS is to Christians. It is the beginning of the Hindu New Year. To celebrate the start of the New Year, people whitewash their homes, open new account books, and buy new clothes. In India men and women wear festive clothes. Many kinds of Diwali delicacies are enjoyed at this time of year. *Jalebis*, pretzels made from flour and butter and coated with sugar, are among many favorite treats. Storytellers speak about Hindu gods, and actors perform scenes from popular tales. *See* HANUKKAH *and* IRANIAN NEW YEAR.

Diwali is marked by bright, spinning, flaring lights—symbols of good fortune and the triumph of good over evil.

Doll Festival

The Doll Festival, Hina Matsuri, is held on March 3 for girls in Japan. It is sometimes referred to as the Peach Blossom Festival because peach trees flower at that time and the fruit symbolizes beauty, gentleness, and peace.

Dolls have a long history in Japan. Thousands of years ago, people rubbed paper dolls over their bodies to absorb evil, then threw them into a river to wash away their misfortunes. Dolls were also placed near children's beds to protect them.

Today people put dolls on special display with specific arrangements. Traditionally, parents present their daughter with a set of dolls on her first birthday. When she is married, the daughter takes the dolls to her new home and eventually passes them on to her own daughters.

On the holiday, families enjoy arranging shelves of dolls. Girls visit each other to admire their dolls. They hold tea parties with rice cakes called *hishi mochi* and other special treats. *See* ADULTS' DAY *and* CHILDREN'S DAY.

Dragon Boat Festival

The Dragon Boat Festival is celebrated in China and by Chinese communities around the world on the fifth day of the fifth moon (around June 21). People considered this month evil and feared that the Dragon God might decide to ruin their crops. To appease the god, the villagers held dragon boat races. These races still take place today.

Dragon boats are long, narrow boats that are elaborately decorated. They have a painted dragon head at the front and a scaly, twisting tail at the back. The longest boats can hold as many as eighty people. Those on shore beat drums and gongs to scare away evil spirits. One man always stands in the front of the boat and throws rice dumplings into the water. *See* DUSSEHRA.

Traditions like the Dragon Boat Festival are celebrated by many Chinese Americans. This dragon boat race was held in Queens, New York.

Dussehra

Dussehra is celebrated for ten days in India during the Hindu lunar month of Asvina, which usually falls during September and October.

Dussehra celebrates the victory of good over evil as told in the *Ramayana,* a sacred Hindu epic. During Dussehra, actors present the Ramlila pageant, which depicts the story of the *Ramayana.* Audiences participate in the events by singing and shouting, "Victory to Rama! Death to Ravana!" The pageant ends with the death of Ravana. Straw dummies, or effigies, of the demon king are stuffed with firecrackers and thrown on fires. The firecrackers explode as the effigies burst into flames.

In West Bengal and by Bengalis throughout India, the festival is celebrated as Durga Puja in honor of the goddess Durga. According to the legend from the *Devimahatmya,* the mighty demon Mahishasura forced all the gods to leave their kingdoms. The gods prayed to Durga and asked for her help. Riding a lion and armed with powerful weapons, Durga easily destroyed Mahishasura. The gods were able to return to their homes.

The first nine days of Durga Puja are spent in prayer. People worship statues of Durga. She is shown as a very tall woman with ten arms. On the tenth day, statues of Durga are carried in a procession to a river or pond for immersion. If possible, the statues are immersed in the Ganges River, which is believed to cure disease and erase the sins of those who bathe in its water. *See* DRAGON BOAT FESTIVAL.

Hindus in Kulu, India, carry a temple god through the street during Dussehra.

Earth Day is celebrated on April 22 around the world.

When the Industrial Revolution began in Europe and the United States in the late eighteenth century, hundreds of factories and mills developed. Up until the mid-1900s, no one thought about how the waste and pollution from those industries were affecting the earth.

A few decades ago, people began to realize what had happened. Lakes and rivers had become unusable because of pollution. People did not have clean drinking water. Acid rain was destroying trees and plants. Entire cities were covered in smog, a combination of smoke and fog. Scientists began talking about "global warming" and other great dangers to our environment.

Everyone can help protect the earth by recycling items like aluminum cans, plastic bottles, and newspapers.

One person who was listening was Gaylord Nelson. He had grown up in Wisconsin with a deep appreciation for nature. He understood that widespread change had to occur to help the earth. Nelson became governor of Wisconsin and promoted many programs to help the environment. Elected to the United States Senate in 1962, he sponsored many laws to help stop pollution.

Nelson developed the idea to devote a day to the earth by talking to students. He persuaded politicians and many other leaders to meet with students to discuss the environment. From these meetings came Earth Day, which was first celebrated on April 22, 1970.

Earth Day was a huge success. People learned about recycling products, how to conserve water, and which products were safe for the environment. Many people rode bikes to work or school to save gas and reduce pollution. Children drew posters about protecting the earth or marched in parades in honor of nature.

The continued observance of Earth Day, along with a growing social awareness, has led to many new laws and practices that protect the earth and have cut down on pollution. *See* ARBOR DAY.

This trash monster is a symbol of people's efforts to fight against waste and pollution.

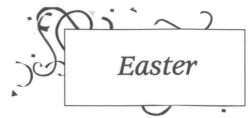

Easter

Easter is celebrated by Christians throughout the world. It always falls on the first Sunday following the first full moon after March 21.

Easter celebrates Jesus' resurrection, or the day he rose from the dead. According to the New Testament, a part of the Christian holy book, the Bible, Jesus spent his life preaching and showing people how they should live. Many powerful people at the time did not believe in God and thought that Jesus was trying to cause trouble. They arrested him and crucified him. Three hours later, Jesus died. He was buried in a tomb that was sealed with a huge rock. Because he had predicted that he would rise from the dead, guards watched to make sure that no one removed the body. Three days after the burial, Jesus' followers went to the tomb. It was empty. Jesus had risen from the dead.

The forty days leading to Easter make up the season of LENT. During this time Christians fast, do penance (show remorse) for their sins, and reflect upon their lives. It is a solemn time as people prepare for Easter.

A popular Easter custom is to watch the sunrise, which is symbolic of rebirth. In Los Angeles, up to 30,000 people gather each year in the Hollywood Bowl—a large open-air theater—to wait for sunrise. After daybreak, everyone attends an outdoor church service. It is a time of happiness and rejoicing.

Early Christians were often baptized, or initiated into the faith, on Easter as a symbol of making a new beginning. People also started a custom of buying new clothes. According to legend, if a young girl wore a new hat on Easter, she would have good luck and find love in the next year. To show off their clothes, people held an Easter parade after church services.

Lamb is one popular main course for Easter dinners. Hundreds of years ago,

A priest displays the chalice and paten, which hold the wine and bread that symbolize the blood and body of Christ. This will be offered to people at Easter Mass.

lambs were used as sacrifices to God. The lamb came to symbolize for Christians the sacrifice that Jesus made for his followers when he died on the cross. Easter dinner customs vary around the world. In Italy people eat bread with hard-boiled eggs baked into it. In Poland the head of the household cuts up a colored egg and passes a piece to everyone at the table. The family says in Polish, "We wish you a happy alleluia," which means "Happy Easter" in English.

One popular Easter tradition is dying hard-boiled eggs with bright colors. In some families, parents hide the eggs for children to find on Easter morning.

Eggs are considered a symbol of new life. In Greece people dye them red, a magical color. They believe that when the red shell is broken, a blessing is released. They also carry eggs with them at Easter. When two people meet, they tap their eggs together. The first person says, "Christ is risen," and the other responds, "He is risen indeed." In Holland, Germany, France, and Switzerland, people create Easter trees as symbols of the resurrection. They place bare branches in pots, hollow out eggs, which they decorate with ribbons, and then hang the eggs from the branches. The branches represent death, whereas the eggs are a symbol of life.

In eighteenth-century France, egg races were popular. People rolled eggs down a hill, and whoever made it to the bottom first won. In the United States, an egg-rolling contest for children is held on Easter Monday at the White House. Easter-egg hunts are also popular. Grown-ups hide eggs and other treats around yards and houses, and children hunt for them.

Legend says that the Easter rabbit leaves the eggs. The story tells of a woman who wanted to buy gifts for her children at Easter but was too poor. Instead she colored eggs and hid them in her yard. When the children were looking for their surprises, a rabbit hopped out from under some bushes. They thought that the rabbit had brought the eggs, so they called it the Easter Bunny. Some people think that rabbits are a symbol of Easter because they have many babies each year and symbolize new life. *See* ASH WEDNESDAY, GOOD FRIDAY, *and* PASSOVER.

Eid al-Adha

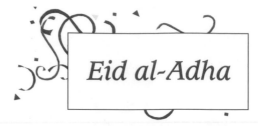

Eid al-Adha, or the Feast of Sacrifice, is held on the tenth day of Dhu al-Hijja, the twelfth month on the Islamic calendar. It is observed in Saudi Arabia, Turkey, Africa, and throughout the Muslim world. It is considered one of the most important feasts of the Muslim faith.

Eid al-Adha is held in honor of Abraham and commemorates a story told in the Koran. One day Allah told Abraham to sacrifice his son Ishmael. (Some scholars believe that Abraham's other son, Isaac, was chosen to be sacrificed.) Because of his great faith and trust in Allah, Abraham believed that Allah had a greater plan than Abraham could see. He reluctantly agreed to sacrifice his son to fulfill Allah's purpose. Just as he was about to kill his son, Allah stopped Abraham and gave him permission to sacrifice a ram in place of his son. Abraham's willingness to sacrifice his son showed the strength of his faith and his desire to obey Allah. Muslims believe that Abraham and his son are the forefathers of the Arab people.

These Muslim women and children will spend the day remembering loved ones who have died, telling stories about Abraham, and praying from the Koran.

During Eid al-Adha, people tell their children stories about Ishmael and Abraham. Traditionally, families recognize Abraham's faith by sacrificing a ram. The ram symbolizes a Muslim's willingness to make sacrifices for Allah. The meat of the ram is typically divided into three parts. One portion is donated to the poor, and the rest is used for a feast with family, friends, and neighbors.

The holy day is also a time to remember the dead, similar to MEMORIAL DAY in the United States. Muslims go to cemeteries, where they tidy and decorate the graves of loved ones and pray for the dead with readings from the Koran. *See* DAY OF THE DEAD.

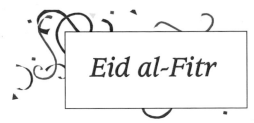

Eid al-Fitr

Eid al-Fitr, also known as the Little Festival or Lesser Feast, is celebrated in Egypt, India, Iran, Iraq, western Africa, Turkey, and throughout the Muslim world. The feast begins on the first day of Shawwal, the tenth month of the Islamic calendar. It lasts for three days.

Eid means "a festival of happiness and a time of great joy" in Arabic. Eid al-Fitr celebrates the end of the month-long fast of RAMADAN. The festivities begin as soon as the new moon is visible, signaling the end of Ramadan. The whole community wears new clothes and recites a special prayer at a large outdoor prayer space called a *musalla*. Then they hold carnivals with rides, games, and puppet shows.

In Turkey the holiday is called the Candy Festival, and children are given candy wrapped in handkerchiefs. All over the Muslim world, people enjoy special treats. A popular food is *shir khorma*, a kind of spaghetti made with milk, sugar, dates, and nuts. It is customary to invite non-Muslim friends to open houses to teach them about the Muslim faith and the holiday. In return, Muslims visit their non-Muslim friends during their major holidays.

Eid al-Fitr is also a time of great generosity. Each household makes an offering to the poor called *al-Fitr*. Traditionally, wealthier Muslims give during Ramadan so that the poor will have money to prepare for the festival. *See* MARDI GRAS.

After the long observance of Ramadan, bright lights, streamers, and festive decorations mark Eid al-Fitr.

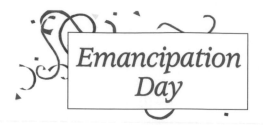

Emancipation Day

Emancipation Day is observed on January 1 in the United States. It commemorates the day President Abraham Lincoln issued the Emancipation Proclamation in 1863.

The plantations of the South grew rapidly in the eighteenth century. Plantation owners needed many people to work the land. They began to use slaves, who were brought from Africa. The Africans were taken against their will, separated from their families, and treated horribly. They became the human property of their owners and lost all rights and freedoms.

Many people, especially in the northern states, disapproved of slavery. Reformers called abolitionists fought to abolish, or eliminate, slavery. They passed out pamphlets, wrote articles, and tried to convince politicians and the general public that all the slaves should be released.

During the Civil War, slavery was a major issue dividing the North and the South. Many slaves ran away to the North to fight for their freedom. Slowly President Lincoln took steps toward freeing the slaves. First he forbade Union officers to return fugitive slaves. Then he declared that the federal government would give money to plantation owners who freed their slaves. Finally on January 1, 1863, he issued the Emancipation Proclamation, which declared:

That on the first day of January, in the year of our Lord one thousand eight hundred and sixty-three, all persons held as slaves within any state or designated part of a state the people whereof shall then be in rebellion against the United States, shall be then, thenceforward, and forever free; and the Executive Government of the United States, including the military and naval authority thereof, will recognize and maintain the freedom of such persons, and will do no act or acts to repress such persons, or any of them, in any efforts they may make for their actual freedom . . .

Although slavery was abolished in 1865, black men were not allowed to vote until 1867. Black women were not allowed to vote until 1920. This picture, entitled "First Vote," appeared on the front page of Harper's Weekly, *a popular journal in the nineteenth century.*

Now, therefore, I, Abraham Lincoln, President of the United States, by virtue of the power in me vested as Commander-in-Chief of the Army and Navy of the United States, in time of actual armed rebellion against the authority and government of the United States, and as a fit and necessary war measure for suppressing said rebellion . . .

This painting symbolizes the power and virtue of the Emancipation Proclamation, with Liberty riding in the powerful chariot.

I do order and declare that all persons held as slaves within said designated States and parts of States are, and henceforward shall be, free; and that the Executive Government of the United States, including the military and naval authorities thereof, shall recognize and maintain the freedom of said persons.

And I hereby enjoin upon the people so declared to be free to abstain from all violence, unless in necessary self-defense; and I recommend to them that, in all cases where allowed, they labor faithfully for reasonable wages.

And I further declare and make known that such persons of suitable condition will be received into the armed service of the United States to garrison forts, positions, stations, and other places, and to man vessels of all sorts in said service.

And upon this act, sincerely believed to be an act of justice, warranted by the Constitution upon military necessity, I invoke the considerate judgment of mankind and the gracious favor of Almighty God.

By the President: Abraham Lincoln
William H. Seward, Secretary of State

Celebrations of Emancipation Day are held mostly in the South. Public readings of the document are held. Students learn about the history of slavery in the United States and work on projects to promote understanding and tolerance. *See* CITIZENSHIP DAY *and* ROBERT E. LEE DAY.

33

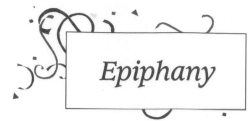

Epiphany

Epiphany is celebrated by Christians around the world on January 6. The word *epiphany* comes from a Greek word meaning "manifestation" or "showing." Centuries ago, this holiday marked the birth of Jesus, the day God manifested himself in the form of his son. In the fourth century, however, CHRISTMAS became the holiday that honored Jesus' birthday, and the meaning of Epiphany changed.

In Europe, North America, and South America, Epiphany commemorates the day the three Magi, or Wise Men, visited Jesus. According to the New Testament in the Bible, on the night of Jesus' birth, the Magi noticed a star that shone brighter than any other. They followed it to the family of Jesus. The Wise Men brought gifts to Jesus: gold, a symbol of royalty; frankincense, a type of incense; and myrrh, a burial spice.

In parts of Europe, three young people are chosen to dress as the Wise Men and lead the community through a Nativity scene. They walk through the streets singing carols and carrying banners. In Spain children wait with gifts to greet the Magi as they travel to Bethlehem.

In the Middle East and the Mediterranean, Epiphany celebrates Jesus' baptism in the Jordan River. In many places, a priest walks around the village, sprinkling holy water on homes. Often a procession follows him from door to door, singing a traditional song. Another custom involves throwing a cross into the sea. Young people dive in after it, and whoever brings it to the surface is presented with gifts.

In Egypt, the water of the Nile River is believed to be at its purest on Epiphany. People store it in special containers and use it throughout the year. People jump into the river three times and drive their cattle into the water to be blessed. In Greece, it is considered bad luck for sailors to be at sea during the twelve days between Christmas and Epiphany. They wait for the waters to be blessed before leaving shore again. *See* ADVENT.

Dressed as a shepherd, this boy holds a lamb for a Nativity play during Epiphany.

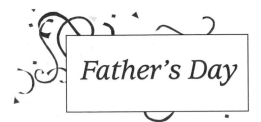

Father's Day

Father's Day is celebrated on the third Sunday in June in the United States and Canada.

The idea for Father's Day came to Sonora Smart Dodd when she heard a sermon in church on MOTHER'S DAY. Her mother had died many years earlier, so Sonora was not able to celebrate with her. However, she thought about all the wonderful things her father had done for his family, raising Sonora and her five brothers and sisters by himself. She decided that there should also be a special day honoring all the fathers in the country.

Sonora took her idea to her church and many other

Father's Day was first celebrated on June 19, 1910, in Spokane, Washington. Today many families celebrate Father's Day by spending it together.

groups in her hometown of Spokane, Washington. People signed petitions and wrote letters to politicians requesting that a special holiday be created for fathers. In Spokane, Father's Day was celebrated in churches, where it was seen as a time to remind fathers of their duty to look after the spiritual welfare of their families. It became customary for people to wear a red rose as a tribute to a father who was living, or a white rose in remembrance of a father who had passed away.

Despite Sonora's efforts, the holiday did not spread beyond Spokane, and by the 1920s, it had died out. It was revived, however, in 1938 when men's clothing retailers saw the sales potential of the holiday. They began a campaign to promote Father's Day with the slogan "Give Dad Something to Wear." Despite the commercial success, it was not until 1972 that Father's Day was proclaimed a nationwide holiday by President Richard Nixon. *See* ADULTS' DAY *and* MOTHER'S DAY.

Flag Day is celebrated on June 14 in the United States. President Harry S. Truman declared it an official holiday in 1949.

The American flag we know today is believed to have been designed by Francis Hopkinson, the New Jersey signer of the Declaration of Independence. A popular legend says that George Washington asked Betsy Ross of Philadelphia to make it. After making a few minor adjustments, such as changing the shape of the stars, she agreed. Although Ross was a seamstress and a flag-maker, most historians do not accept this story as fact.

Each part of the flag's design has special meaning. The white stars on the blue background represent the states in the union. As the number of states increased throughout the nation's history, so did the number of stars on the flag. The thirteen stripes symbolize the thirteen original colonies. The red stripes represent England, and the white stripes represent the United States. The white and red stripes alternate to show America's independence from England.

The American flag is the only one in the world to have had a national anthem—"The Star-Spangled Banner"—written about it. Francis Scott Key wrote a poem that was inspired by the flag flying over Fort McHenry in Baltimore, Maryland, after a bombardment during the War of 1812. Key's poem was later set to music and adopted as America's national anthem.

On Flag Day, Americans fly the flag in front of homes, schools, and businesses. Students learn how the flag should be treated and participate in flag-raising ceremonies. People sing "The Star-Spangled Banner" and recite the Pledge of Allegiance. *See* INDEPENDENCE DAY.

The first American flag is shown here being made by Betsy Ross, a seamstress who lived in Philadelphia during the time of the Revolutionary War.

Fourth of July

See INDEPENDENCE DAY.

Full Moon Day

Full Moon Day, or Magha Puja, is celebrated on the night of the full moon during the Hindu month of Magha. The Buddhist calendar is similar to the Hindu calendar but uses a different moon to begin the New Year. This holiday usually occurs in February. Buddhists around the world observe this important holy day.

The holiday commemorates the time when 1,250 disciples of the Buddha met at the Veluvan Monastery in Rajagriha, India. They had not planned the meeting. Each person felt the need to go to the monastery. When they arrived, they listened to the Buddha preach about the monastic regulations and predict his death and entry into Nirvana, which is the highest state of bliss and well-being. Buddhists pray and behave virtuously in hope of achieving Nirvana.

On Full Moon Day, sermons about the Buddha and the attainment of Nirvana are preached in the temples. Monks meet together to pray and chant. People spend the day doing good deeds, such as offering food to the poor and freeing captive animals. When the sun sets, the monks walk around the temples three times carrying flowers, incense, and candles in honor of the Buddha. *See* VESAK.

This Tibetan Bonpo monk performs a ritual dance for the Full Moon Festival at the Gamel Monastery in Tibet.

Ganesha Carturthi

Ganesha Carturthi is celebrated on the fourth day of the Hindu month Bhadrapada, which falls during August and September. The holiday celebrates the birth of the god Ganesha.

Ganesha is one of the most important Hindu gods. According to legend, the goddess Parvati created Ganesha one morning before her bath and had him stand guard outside the bathhouse. When Parvati's husband, Shiva, wanted to enter, Ganesha barred him. Shiva did not realize who Ganesha was and became so angry that he cut off Ganesha's head. When Parvati saw what had happened, she was overwhelmed with grief. To console her, Shiva sent a messenger to find a new head for Ganesha. The first creature the messenger saw was an elephant, and he brought back its head. That is why Ganesha is depicted with an elephant head. He is also shown riding on a rat and has a big potbelly, which symbolizes good harvests and plenty of food. One day when he was young, Ganesha ate a lot of pudding called *modakas.* Soon after, the rat he was riding on became startled by a snake. Ganesha fell off, and his stomach burst open. He stuffed the pudding back in and tied his belly together with the snake.

Before trying a task, Hindus pray to Ganesha to remove any obstacles that may be in the path of success. Almost every home has an image of Ganesha over the doorway to bring good fortune. On his birthday, worshipers pray to Ganesha and make offerings of *modakas.* They carry images of him through the streets and immerse them in a river or the sea. In farming communities, people take clay or silt from the river and spread it on the fields. *See* DIWALI *and* DUSSEHRA.

A statue of Ganesha, the Hindu god of good fortune, is carried down a street by people celebrating his birthday.

Good Friday

Good Friday is celebrated on the Friday before EASTER throughout the Christian world.

Good Friday commemorates the day that Jesus was nailed to the cross. In Catholic churches, the altar is completely bare on this day. All the statues are covered with mourning cloths. People pray at the Stations of the Cross, which are fourteen images that tell the story of the trial, judgment, and crucifixion of Jesus. The stations are usually represented by paintings or carvings on the wall. People walk slowly from station to station, saying specific prayers for each image.

A three-hour service is held in many churches. Lasting from noon to three o'clock, it represents the time Jesus hung on the cross. The service focuses on the seven things Jesus said before he died. The service was first performed in Peru after an earthquake struck Lima in 1687. *See* ASH WEDNESDAY *and* CHRISTMAS.

Guy Fawkes Day

Guy Fawkes Day, also known as Bonfire Night, is celebrated on November 5 in England. The day commemorates the foiling of a plot by a famous traitor, Guy Fawkes.

In 1605, many people were unhappy with the way King James I of England treated Catholics. Some of them came up with a plan to blow up Parliament, the king, and the queen. They placed thirty-six barrels of gunpowder in the cellar of the Parliament building and chose Fawkes to set off the explosion. The Gunpowder Plot failed because one of the conspirators was scared and warned Parliament. Fawkes was caught, and everyone involved was arrested and executed.

On Guy Fawkes Day, people remember the failed Gunpowder Plot. The yeomen of the guard reenact the event by dressing in traditional costumes and searching the cellar of the House of Parliament. During the day, children make straw dummies named "guys" and walk the streets begging for "a penny for the guy." That night, the guys are burned in bonfires. Fireworks fill the night sky to complete the celebration. *See* BASTILLE DAY.

To celebrate Guy Fawkes Day, this brave man reenacts the tragic plot in which Guy Fawkes played a part.

Halloween is observed on October 31 in the United States and the United Kingdom.

The ancient Celtic harvest festival, Samhain, was the earliest version of Halloween. About 3,000 years ago, the Celts believed in many gods and worshiped nature. They thought that the spirits of the recently deceased traveled together to the land of the dead on Samhain. To win the favor of the spirits, people sacrificed crops and animals, and wore costumes and masks to disguise themselves. In Scotland farmers carried torches around their fields to frighten evil spirits away from the crops. In Wales people built bonfires on hilltops and carefully watched them until midnight. When the fire burned out, everyone ran down the hill as fast as possible. It was thought that the devil would capture the last person down the hill.

After the Roman invasion of Britain in A.D.43, Samhain was linked with Roman autumn holidays. The Romans celebrated a harvest festival in honor of the goddess Pomona, from which came many customs associated with apples and nuts. They also celebrated Feralia, a day to honor the dead. Halloween is linked to all three of these holidays.

As Christianity spread throughout Europe, pagan holidays were given new Christian interpretations. Samhain, Feralia, and Pomona were combined into ALL SOULS' DAY. The night before this holiday was known as All Hallows' E'en. *Hallow* is an old word meaning "holy," and *e'en* is Scottish for "evening." Eventually it became one word—Halloween.

In 1484, Pope Innocent VIII outlawed these ancient religions. He said that they were connected with witchcraft. Witches still play a large role in the traditions of Halloween. After their religions were outlawed, believers met secretly in the woods at night and wore black clothes to avoid being seen. Halloween was one of two nights during the year when witches

Wearing Halloween costumes to trick-or-treat can be great fun. Children attend Halloween parties, where they play games and eat lots of candy!

were believed to gather. People believed that on Halloween, witches flew on broomsticks, danced on hilltops, cast spells, and played tricks on people.

Most of the customs associated with Halloween were brought to the United States by Irish immigrants in the 1800s. The trick-or-treat tradition began in Ireland. On Halloween, beggars would go to the homes of rich people and ask for food and money as gifts for Muck Olla, a god who rewarded the generous and punished the stingy. Most people feared Muck Olla and "treated" the beggars rather than be "tricked" by the god.

Carving jack-o'-lanterns is also an old Irish custom. There is a legend about a selfish man named Jack. When he died, he could not get into heaven. He could not get into hell either, because during his life he had played many tricks on the devil. His spirit was forced to roam the countryside forever, with only a small lantern to guide the way. In honor of Jack, English children carry small lanterns made from beets called punkies. In Scotland they are made from turnips and called bogies. In America jack-o'-lanterns are made out of carved pumpkins.

Wearing costumes is still a popular tradition, but it is done for fun, not to hide from evil spirits. Black cats, bats, and witches were once thought to have supernatural, evil powers. Now pictures of them are used as decorations. Black and orange are seen everywhere during Halloween. Orange symbolizes autumn and the harvest, and black is the color of death and darkness. The colors remind us that Halloween was once a harvest festival and a festival of the dead. *See* DRAGON BOAT FESTIVAL *and* KWANZAA.

People carve all kinds of faces on jack-o'-lanterns: happy, sad, funny, and best of all, really scary ones!

Besides serving as jack-o'-lanterns, pumpkins are used for food and decoration. Pumpkin pie and roasted pumpkin seeds are very popular treats.

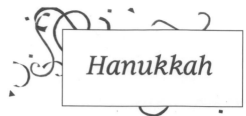

Hanukkah

Hanukkah is celebrated for eight days on the Jewish calendar, from Kislev 25 to Tebeth 2, all over the world. These days fall sometime between November 25 and December 26.

Hanukkah, which commemorates a military victory by the Jewish people, is also known as the Festival of Lights. Thousands of years ago, Israel was ruled by Syrians. The Syrians followed the Greek religion. They worshiped many gods, whereas the Jews worshiped only one God. One Syrian ruler, Antiochus IV, decreed that the Jewish people should worship the Greek gods. He destroyed Jewish temples and erected statues of Greek gods. He demanded that the Jewish people break their dietary laws. All Jews were ordered to pray to the Greek gods. Fearing for their lives, many people obeyed. Those who refused were killed.

One family, the Maccabees, refused to worship the Greek gods. When the king's troops came to their village of Mod'im, Mattathias Maccabee and his five sons refused to do as they were told. When the commander of the troops ordered them to eat foods forbidden by their religion, they refused and killed all the Syrian troops. Then they fled into the hills, and many other Jews followed them. They built up a great army and returned to the city to destroy the Greek statues and encourage Jews to keep their faith. The Maccabees and their followers fought four major battles against the Syrians. They lost the first three but won the last.

After the battle, Judah Maccabee, one of Mattathias's sons, led his followers back into Jerusalem. They tore down the statues of Greek gods and rededicated the Temple to God. Their celebration is considered the first Hanukkah. When they dedicated the Temple, the Maccabees wanted to light the menorah, a lamp that has places for seven

Families often exchange gifts, play the dreidel game, and eat special holiday foods for Hanukkah

candles or seven portions of lamp oil. According to legend, they had only enough oil to light the menorah for one day. By a miracle, the oil in the menorah stayed lit for eight days. That is why the holiday lasts for eight days. Judah and his brothers declared Hanukkah a yearly holiday to celebrate their defeat of the Syrians.

The menorah is the most important symbol of Hanukkah; however, today's Hanukkah menorahs are different from the original seven-branched ones. Now it is called the *hanukkiyah*, and it has branches for nine candles. Eight of the candles represent the days of Hanukkah. The ninth candle is the *shammesh*, or servant. It is responsible for lighting all the other candles. On the first night of Hanukkah, the *shammesh* lights the candle farthest to the right. Each night another candle is lit. On the last night, all nine candles burn.

Some families give gifts on all eight days. However, most people set aside one day of the holiday for exchanging gifts. Small gifts of money, called Hanukkah *gelt,* are popular. Children often use the gelt to play dreidel, a traditional game. A dreidel is a top with a Hebrew letter on each of its four sides. The letters stand for "*Nes gadol hayah sham,*" which means "A great miracle happened there." This refers to the miracle of the oil at the rededication of the Temple. Each letter is assigned a value. When the top stops spinning, the player gets the amount of points given to the letter it stops on.

Usually one day is set aside for a Hanukkah party. Traditional food is served. Latkes, a type of potato pancake, are typically served with applesauce and sugar or sour cream. At the Hanukkah party, people sing songs and play games. Spinning the dreidel is a favorite game. *See* CHRISTMAS, DIWALI, *and* KWANZAA.

These children perform an important part of the Hanukkah tradition: lighting the candles on the hanukkiyah.

Holocaust Remembrance Day

Holocaust Remembrance Day, or Yom Hashoah, is observed on the twenty-seventh day of the Jewish month Nisan (between April 8 and May 6). The word *holocaust* means "widespread destruction by fire." It is used to describe the murder of six million Jews during World War II.

In 1933, Adolf Hitler became the leader of Germany. The dictator quickly began his horrifying plan to destroy all Jewish people.

On September 1, 1939, Germany invaded Poland. France and Great Britain declared war on Germany, and World War II began. The countries that united against Germany and its supporters were called Allies.

By 1940, Germany controlled most of Europe. Jews were segregated into ghettos, where they were forced to live in small, crowded rooms with no running

Former inmates of the concentration camp at Ebensee, Austria, leave the camp after being freed by the U.S. Third Army. The sign reads, "We welcome our liberators."

water, heat, or electricity. Hunger and disease killed thousands of people. From the ghettos, the Jews were taken to concentration camps. Millions of people were starved, forced to work in inhumane conditions, and killed in gas chambers.

In 1945, Allied troops entered Germany and liberated the inmates of the concentration camps. By the end of the war, one-third of the Jewish people in the world had been murdered.

The Knesset, or parliament, in Israel established Holocaust Remembrance Day on the anniversary of the Allied liberation of the first concentration camp, in Buchenwald, Germany. On Holocaust Remembrance Day in Israel, a siren sounds throughout the country, and people observe two minutes of silent reflection. Candlelight ceremonies are held. The poems, writings, and artwork of Holocaust victims are displayed. Students study the Holocaust and read books such as *The Diary of Anne Frank*. People visit memorials that have been established all over the world. *See* MARTIN LUTHER KING JR. DAY *and* PASSOVER.

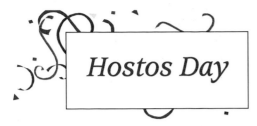

Hostos Day

Hostos Day is celebrated on January 11 in Puerto Rico. It commemorates the birth of Eugenio María de Hostos in 1839. Hostos was a philosopher and great patriot. He became politically active while he was a student in Spain. He believed that Puerto Rico, a Spanish colony, should be given independence from Spain. He also protested against African slavery in Cuba and Puerto Rico, and the exploitation of Chinese immigrants in Peru. Hostos left Spain in 1869 when the new constitution failed to recognize Puerto Rico as an independent country. Over the course of his career, Hostos was an active participant in the Cuban independence movement. He edited a Cuban independence newspaper in the United States, traveled throughout South America, and taught in Chile, where he fought for educational opportunities for women. After the Spanish-American War in 1898, the United States took control of Puerto Rico. The U.S. government rejected Hostos's proposal for an independent Puerto Rico.

As director of the Central College and inspector of public education in the Dominican Republic, Hostos worked to reorganize the educational system. He died on August 11, 1903.

During the years before his death, he wrote *History of Teaching, Comments on the Science of Teaching*, and *Reform in the Teaching of Law*. Hostos Community College in the Bronx, New York, is named for him.

On Hostos Day, people in Latin American communities in North America, South America, and the Caribbean reflect on the positive changes for which Eugenio María de Hostos worked so long and hard. *See* JAMHURI DAY *and* MARTIN LUTHER KING JR. DAY.

Although it was created in 1895, the Puerto Rican flag was not officially adopted by the government until 1952.

Independence Day (Fourth of July)

Independence Day is celebrated on July 4 in the United States. It is considered the birthday of the United States of America.

The holiday commemorates the signing of the Declaration of Independence on July 4, 1776. Until then, the thirteen American colonies were ruled by England. The colonists had to obey laws they considered unfair and pay heavy taxes on items such as tea, spices, and cloth. They had no vote in the government. "No taxation without representation" became a common demand.

In 1774, the leaders of several colonies met in Philadelphia to solve their problems with England. The meeting was called the Continental Congress, and great political leaders such as John Adams and George Washington participated. Seven months later, in 1775, the Continental Congress met again and decided to fight for independence rather than accept British rule. In 1776 the Revolutionary War began. The British army was well trained and had ample supplies and weapons. The colonists were not trained soldiers. They lacked good weapons and clothing to keep them warm in the winter, but they fought hard because they believed in America's right to be a free country, independent from England.

The Continental Congress continued to meet during the war. The members agreed that they wanted to govern themselves and make their own laws, but they discussed and debated many different ways to accomplish their goal. Thomas Jefferson wrote down ideas for

a new form of government. Finally after many debates, the Continental Congress approved Jefferson's outline. This document, called the Declaration of Independence, states that all men are created equal and have a right to life, liberty, and the pursuit of happiness. It also says that the government must protect the rights of the people.

The Statue of Liberty symbolizes America's independence and the freedom the country offers to all who enter. France gave it to the United States in 1886. The statue was shipped in 214 crates and assembled on Bedloe's Island, later renamed Liberty Island, in New York Harbor.

When the Declaration was signed and printed, crowds of people celebrated. Ships fired thirteen cannonballs in honor of the thirteen colonies. Bands played, parades lined the streets, and church bells rang in every colony. When the Declaration was read in Philadelphia, people rang the Liberty Bell, which was originally used to call public officials to meetings. Now it is a symbol of America's freedom. Seven years after the Declaration was written, the colonists won the war against England and were free of English rule.

For a Fourth of July parade, this clown is dressed up as Uncle Sam, a national symbol of the United States. Uncle Sam was created in 1813 but became popular as part of an armed forces recruitment poster during World War I.

Many patriotic symbols are associated with America and the Fourth of July. One is the bald eagle, the national bird of the United States. Benjamin Franklin wanted the turkey to be the national bird. He thought that the eagle represented a lack of morals because it stole food from weaker birds. Congress disagreed and chose the bald eagle, a species of bird found only in North America. Today the bald eagle appears on coins, stamps, dollar bills, and the great seal of the United States.

On the Fourth of July, there are parades in most cities and towns. The first such parade took place in the 1820s in Washington, D.C. President John Quincy Adams led a group of dignitaries up the Potomac River on steamboats and barges. Today there are marching bands and floats with patriotic themes. Veterans' organizations march in uniform, and students march with school groups and other youth organizations. People have picnics with their families and friends. Children play games, run relay races, and dress up in colonial-style clothing. After dark, towns have huge fireworks displays, emphasizing the colors of the flag—red, white, and blue. *See* CENTRAL AFRICAN REPUBLIC INDEPENDENCE DAY, TEXAS INDEPENDENCE DAY, *and* MEXICAN INDEPENDENCE DAY.

Iranian New Year (Nawruz)

The Iranian New Year occurs on the vernal equinox (March 20, 21, or 22) of each year. The holiday lasts for thirteen days and celebrates the transition from winter to spring and the beginning of the New Year. It is called *Nawruz*, which means "new year" in Persian.

To begin the year well, people buy new clothes and give a good spring cleaning to their homes. On the night before Nawruz begins, families eat omelets and pilaf, a rice dish, symbolizing the good fortune they hope to enjoy the following year.

Nawruz comes from traditions rooted in the Zoroastrian belief system. Zoroastrianism was the religion of ancient Persia before Islam became popular 1,400 years ago. These people would begin their celebrations five days before the New Year began. They lit bonfires on their rooftops to signal the guardian angels that humans were ready to greet them. They called this the Suri Festival.

In Iran, people still do their spring cleaning and hold elaborate banquets during Nawruz. They serve seven foods that begin with the letter S to symbolize the seven creations and the seven holy mortals who protect them. These foods include the following: sumac (*somagh*), apples (*sib*), jujube fruit (*senjed*), garlic (*seer*), hyacinth (*sonbol*), a wheat germ dish (*samanon*), and sprouted seeds (*sabzeh*).

On the thirteenth day of Nawruz, it is considered unlucky to stay at home. People take picnics to the countryside and spend the day with

family and friends. Singers, clowns, dancers, and actors entertain in the parks. Children grow plants from wheat seeds and drop the plants into streams. This is a way of "throwing away" bad luck so that the New Year can begin with peace and good fortune. *See* ROSH HASHANAH, VAISAKHI, *and* VERNAL EQUINOX.

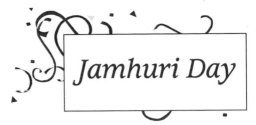

Jamhuri Day

Jamhuri Day is observed in Kenya on December 12. It celebrates Kenya's independence from Great Britain. *Jamhuri* means "gathering" in Swahili.

In the 1800s, the British took control of Kenya. They forced Kenyans off their land and exploited the natural resources. The British became very wealthy, but the Kenyans grew poor.

In the 1920s, the Kenyans began to rebel against the British. Jomo Kenyatta became a leader of the effort. He spoke out for African rights. In 1952 the Kenyans staged a huge rebellion. Many Kenyans and British

Jomo Kenyatta was a longtime leader of the independence movement in Kenya. He was arrested in 1952 and imprisoned until 1961, two years before Kenya was granted independence. He became the first prime minister of Kenya in 1963.

were killed, and Kenyatta was arrested. This act angered the Kenyans, and more violence erupted between the Kenyan people and British and colonial troops. Eventually the British began to listen to the Kenyans' demands. On December 12, 1963, Britain granted Kenya independence.

Jamhuri Day is the most important holiday in Kenya. People shout "*uhuru!*" which means "freedom!" in Swahili. Political leaders remind Kenyans of the fight for independence. Jets fly overhead while military troops march in formation. People perform *ngomas,* traditional folk dances, and children's choirs sing traditional songs. *See* CENTRAL AFRICAN REPUBLIC INDEPENDENCE DAY, HOSTOS DAY, *and* INDEPENDENCE DAY.

Feast of Joan of Arc

The feast day of Joan of Arc is observed on May 30 by Catholic communities around the world, especially in France.

Joan grew up during the early 1400s in a small village in northern France. At the time, France was at war with England. When Joan was fourteen years old, she heard the voices of Saints Catherine, Margaret, and Michael telling her that she had to save France from England. Joan led an army to fight the English. She won many victories, but she was captured and charged with heresy and witchcraft. She was burned at the stake on May 30, 1431. In 1920, the Catholic Church declared Joan a saint. She is honored on the anniversary of her death. *See* PULASKI DAY, ROBERT E. LEE DAY, *and* ST. PATRICK'S DAY.

King Kamehameha I Day

King Kamehameha I Day is celebrated in Hawaii on June 11. It is the only public holiday in the United States that honors royalty.

In the 1700s, the Hawaiian Islands were ruled by many chiefs, called *aliis*. Kamehameha I was born in 1758, the son of a chief. *Kamehameha* means "the lonely one" in Hawaiian.

In 1778 Kamehameha served as an aide to his uncle, who ruled Hawaii, the largest of the islands. When the uncle died, he left his kingdom to his son, Kiwalao, who was killed later that year. Kamehameha fought with two other chiefs for control of the island. Eventually he won and soon controlled all eight Hawaiian Islands.

As the first person to rule all of Hawaii, Kamehameha brought peace and prosperity to the kingdom. He established trade with other countries and allowed the islands to be used as a rest stop for ships and sailors. He also made important changes in the customs of his land. He created the *mamalahoe kanawai,* or "law of the splintered paddle," which protected common people from brutal rulers. He outlawed human sacrifice. He was also able to preserve many traditional Hawaiian laws, customs, and religious beliefs. Kamehameha died on the island of Hawaii on May 8, 1819. His son, Liholiho, became the new king—Kamehameha II.

In 1898 the islands were annexed by the United States. On June 14, 1900, Hawaii became a U.S. territory. All Hawaiian citizens became American citizens. In 1959 the overwhelming majority of Hawaiian people voted for Hawaii to become an American state, which it did on August 21. The history and culture of Hawaii are very important to Hawaiians. That is why they celebrate a king even though Hawaii is part of a democratic country.

Festivities honoring Kamehameha last for several days. Leis—Hawaiian necklaces made of flowers—are draped over statues of Kamehameha. Parades feature elaborately decorated floats, men representing the king in feather cloaks and headresses, and princesses on horseback wearing the *pa'u,* or brightly colored satin riding dresses. There are also arts-and-crafts fairs, hula dancing, and luaus, or traditional Hawaiian cookouts. *See* VICTORIA DAY.

This statue of King Kamehameha I stares out over the land to which he brought peace and prosperity.

Korean New Year

These members of the Little Angels, a Korean children's dance group, are performing during a New Year's Day celebration.

In Korea the New Year is celebrated twice, once in the lunar calendar and once in the solar calendar. On the solar calendar, the New Year begins on January 1; on the lunar calendar, it falls on the first day of the first moon in the new lunar year.

On New Year's Eve, people light torches in their homes and stay up late to defend the New Year from evil spirits. At midnight, people make lots of noise and celebrate. In the capital city of Seoul, they ring the church bells as soon as the clock strikes midnight.

To start the year off well, Koreans repay any debts they have and thoroughly clean their homes. Then they dress in traditional clothes and visit friends and relatives. Children often receive new clothes. Families prepare special meals. A traditional holiday food is a soup called *ttokkuk,* or rice cake soup. The rice cakes are made of a sticky rice called *ttok,* and the soup is made of rice cakes, pheasant, chicken, pine nuts, and chestnuts.

Children play many games on New Year's Day. Boys fly uniquely shaped kites with long tails. Sometimes they paste glass powder on the strings to try to cut the strings of other kites. They work to pull and tug their own kites out of danger while trying to cut down others. The winner is the boy whose kite is last in the sky.

Girls often play on wide seesaws built low to the ground. This tradition goes back to a time when ladies were forbidden to leave their courtyards. The young women would stand on seesaws and jump up to see over the garden walls.

Lunar New Year's Day is a time to remember and honor ancestors. Families gather in the home of their eldest member to hold memorial services. They offer foods such as rice, fruit, meat, and wine to their ancestors by placing them in front of their photographs. Each person bows to the ancestors, then to his or her elders. *See* CHINESE NEW YEAR, NEW YEAR'S DAY, *and* VIETNAMESE NEW YEAR.

51

Krishna's Birthday

Krishna's birthday, Janmastami, is celebrated on the eighth day of the Hindu month Bhadrapada, which usually occurs around August or September. *Janma* means "birth," and *astami* means "eighth."

Krishna is one of the most popular Hindu gods. Hindus believe that the gods can transform themselves into humans or animals to help people in need. Krishna is a form of the powerful god Vishnu. Hindus believe that Vishnu appeared as a fish, tortoise, boar, man-lion, dwarf, son of a sage (wise man), and prince. Krishna was his eighth avatar, or form. Krishna's mission was to rid the world of Kamsa, a tyrannical king who was the son of a demon. Kamsa had imprisoned the real king to steal the throne. He brought harm to good people and helped the evil ones prosper.

According to legend, Krishna was raised by the herdsmen of Gokul. He loved to dance with girls and play his flute in the forest. He destroyed many evil demons and performed various magical acts. There are many other stories telling about Krishna's life. The epic, or long and dramatic poem, *Mahabharata* describes a few of his adventures. Another text, the *Bhagavad-gita*, outlines his views on duty and life.

To celebrate Krishna's birthday, Hindus play music, dance, sing religious songs, and recite selections from the epics describing Krishna's life. Children make footprints out of flour and water. They place the prints so that they lead from the front door to the meditation room. The footprints show that Krishna was in the house. Everyone fasts for twenty-four hours on this day. At midnight when the fast is over, people ring bells, clang cymbals, and blow horns in celebration. People often eat dairy products after the fast because Krishna liked milk and butter when he was a child. People bathe statues of Krishna in milk. *See* CHRISTMAS, CONFUCIUS'S BIRTHDAY, *and* MUHAMMAD'S BIRTHDAY.

The Hindu god, Krishna, is depicted here playing a flute with his brother, Balarama.

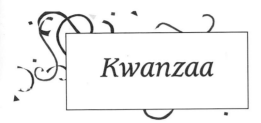

Kwanzaa

The seven candles in a kinara are displayed on a woven straw mat called a mekeka. Fruit and vegetables representing the harvest are also placed on the mekeka. A family places an ear of corn on the display for each child. The last item on the mat is the unity cup, a goblet from which each member of the family drinks, symbolizing the unity of the family and the community.

African Americans celebrate Kwanzaa from December 26 to January 1. Dr. Maulana Karenga of Nigeria, a professor at the University of California at Los Angeles, created the holiday in 1966. Believing that African Americans were losing touch with their African heritage, he decided to promote African culture. Karenga studied various harvest festivals celebrated by different peoples in Africa and decided to create a similar celebration. He named the new holiday *Kwanzaa*, which means "first fruits" in Swahili.

The number seven has great significance in many African cultures, so Karenga made it an important feature of the holiday. The name Kwanzaa has seven letters, the celebration lasts for seven days, and people reflect upon seven principles. Each day is devoted to one of these principles: unity *(umoja)*, self-determination *(kujichagulia)*, collective work and responsibility *(ujima)*, cooperative economics *(ujamma)*, creativity *(kuumba)*, purpose *(nia)*, and faith *(imani)*. A candle is lit for each principle and placed in a seven-branched holder called a *kinara*. The candles are red, black, and green, symbolizing the struggle of African Americans and hope for good fortune in the future. Red stands for the blood of the people. Black is for the people and the deep well of their ancestors. Green symbolizes a promising future for the people.

The night before the last day of Kwanzaa, communities hold feasts called *karamu*. Each family brings a dish to share. At the dinner, people perform in plays and give speeches on African culture, traditions, and beliefs. Most people wear traditional African clothing, which is usually very colorful with bright, elaborate designs.

On the last day of Kwanzaa, January 1, adults give gifts to children. The gifts tend to focus on the African American community and emphasize the spirit of giving rather than receiving. The final day is also used to make resolutions for the year ahead. *See* CHRISTMAS *and* HANUKKAH.

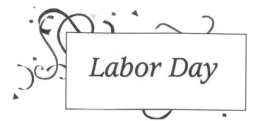

Labor Day

Labor Day is celebrated on the first Monday of September. It honors workers in the United States, Canada, Puerto Rico, and the Virgin Islands.

In the 1800s, the Industrial Revolution changed the types of jobs people held. The invention of new machines meant that people were needed to work in mills and factories instead of farming or working in small shops. They began to move to cities. The conditions at work were dangerous, and people were often seriously injured. They also worked long hours for little pay and seldom had a day off.

The workers knew that these conditions were unfair, yet if they complained, they lost their jobs. However, they understood the power of unity. Carpenters, machinists, bricklayers, and many other groups of workers formed unions. Factory owners often had to listen when their employees went on strike or refused to work until conditions improved.

In 1882 Peter J. McGuire, a carpenter and labor union leader, decided that a holiday should be held to celebrate the unions' many successes and to honor the workers. The Central Labor Union of New York City liked the idea and helped organize a festival in Union Square on September 5. McGuire chose that date because it filled the wide gap between INDEPENDENCE DAY and THANKSGIVING. More than ten thousand workers marched in a huge parade, picnicked, and watched fireworks.

The day was a great success. News of the festival traveled to other cities, and by 1893, thirty states held their own celebrations. In 1894 President Grover Cleveland made Labor Day an official national holiday.

Today Labor Day is still an important holiday. Offices close, and most workers have the day off. Celebrations are held all over the country. For children, Labor Day usually marks the end of summer and the beginning of the new school year. *See* MAY DAY.

Labor Day weekend symbolizes the end of summer, even though summer officially ends weeks later. Many families celebrate Labor Day with summer activities, such as going to the beach.

54

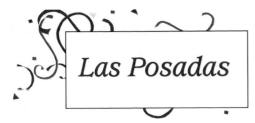

Las Posadas

Las Posadas is celebrated for nine days, from December 16 to 24, in Mexico and parts of the United States with large Mexican American populations.

Las Posadas is a reenactment of the night of the birth of Jesus. Families walk around their neighborhoods seeking shelter in the way that Mary, the mother of Jesus, and her husband, Joseph, did. Finally on the last day, Christmas Eve, they are offered lodging, as Mary and Joseph were. Everyone enters a house and celebrates.

An altar is prepared depicting the Nativity, or birth scene, with the figures of Mary and Joseph and the infant Jesus. A favorite game for children is the piñata, a papier-mâché figure that hangs from the ceiling or a tree branch. Children are blindfolded and take turns trying to break the piñata open with a stick. When it breaks, candy and toys fall to the ground, and everyone scrambles to get their share. *See* CHRISTMAS *and* EPIPHANY.

The festivities on this widely celebrated holiday include dances, feasts, and games for children. Children take turns trying to break open a piñata so that they can collect the candy inside.

Leap Year Day

Leap Year Day occurs on February 29 in countries that use the Gregorian calendar. These countries are found on every continent. The day appears on the calendar only once every four years.

According to the Gregorian calendar, the standard year has 365 days of twenty-four hours each. However, it actually takes Earth about five hours longer to revolve around the sun. To make up the difference and get the calendar back in line with the sun, an extra day is added to the month of February every four years. If the year ends in 00, the extra day is added only if the year is divisible by 400. For instance, the years 1200 and 1600 had February 29, but 1700 and 1900 did not.

It is called Leap Year Day because the early English courts did not recognize the existence of an extra day. They would "leap" over it in the record books. People born on Leap Year Day can joke that they get one year older only every four years. *See* APRIL FOOLS' DAY.

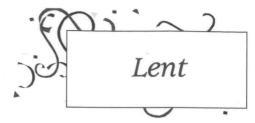

Lent

The Lenten season is made up of the forty days before EASTER and is observed in Christian communities throughout the world. Forty is a symbolic number in Christianity. According to the Bible, Moses spent forty days on Mount Sinai, and Jesus spent forty days in the desert. Lent is a time of preparation for the coming of Easter. The word *Lent* comes from an Anglo-Saxon word meaning "spring."

Many years ago, the focus of Lent was on physical suffering as a form of penitence, or regret for sins. People had to fast; they could not eat or drink except for one small meal late in the evening consisting only of certain foods. Beginning in the nineteenth century, the rules regarding the fast were loosened. Fish and eggs were allowed, and the small meal was moved to an earlier part of the day. Today fasting is not a common practice. Instead, Lent focuses more on spiritual preparation and penitence. People try to simplify their lives, giving up some extra things to practice sacrifice and to concentrate on prayer. Children may give up eating candy, watching television, or playing video games for Lent.

In the fifth century, people shaped dough into two crossed arms to remind themselves of the importance of prayer. The bread was called "little arms," or *bracellae.* Today we know it as the pretzel.

During Lent people pray, ask God to forgive their sins, and reflect on the meaning of their faith. Many holy days are observed during the forty days. The day before Lent begins is called Shrove Tuesday or MARDI GRAS. It is a time of celebration and feasting as people prepare for the hardships of Lent. Lent begins on ASH WEDNESDAY, a day when people go to church and

For many people, giving up sweets is a way of showing devotion, penitence, and discipline during Lent.

ask forgiveness for their sins. As a sign of their repentance, the priest marks on observers the symbol of the cross with ashes. The fourth Sunday of Lent is called Mothering Sunday. This used to be a day when servants returned to their own homes so that they could go to the church where they grew up, in their "mother church."

Prayer is an important part of the forty days of Lent.

The last week of Lent is called Holy Week, during which Christians remember the events that led up to the crucifixion of Jesus. Holy Week begins with PALM SUNDAY, which commemorates Jesus' entry into Jerusalem. It is said that people spread branches on the ground and waved palm fronds to welcome him. Thursday of this week is called Maundy Thursday or Holy Thursday. *Maundy* means "command." The Bible says that on this night, Jesus ate the Last Supper with his disciples and commanded them to love one another. Later in the night, Jesus was arrested and taken away. The next day is GOOD FRIDAY, which commemorates the day Jesus died on the cross. Christians believe that Jesus rose from the dead three days later. This miraculous event is celebrated with EASTER, the end of the Lenten season.

See CHRISTMAS *and* RAMADAN.

This bread is reminiscent of the fifth-century bracellae, bread that looked like crossed arms to symbolize the importance of prayer.

57

Mardi Gras

Mardi Gras, which means "Fat Tuesday" in French, occurs on the Tuesday before LENT. Lent is a long period of fasting and penitence, and Mardi Gras is a day of fun before the more serious days of Lent begin. The weeks leading up to Mardi Gras are a time of great excitement as people prepare for the holiday. Mardi Gras, also called Carnival, is celebrated in many countries, including the United States, Brazil, and several of the Caribbean islands.

In England the day is called Pancake Tuesday, and numerous stacks of pancakes are eaten. People cook pancakes until all their butter, milk, and eggs are gone. In Germany it is called Fastnacht, or "Eve of the Fast." People bake large rectangular doughnuts filled with molasses and dunk them in tea.

The tradition of Mardi Gras dates back to ancient European spring festivals for the fertility of crops and livestock. "Fat Tuesday" refers to a tradition of parading a fat ox through the streets in hopes of a prosperous year. These traditions were brought to America in 1699 when French settlers landed at the mouth of the Mississippi River. They named the area Point du Mardi Gras because they knew that their loved ones in France were celebrating Mardi Gras on that day. Nineteen years later, New Orleans, Louisiana, was founded near the Point du Mardi Gras. New Orleans is where the biggest Mardi Gras celebrations in the United States take place. Brazil is home to another version of Mardi Gras called Carnival.

Mardi Gras was celebrated in the Christian countries of Europe long before New Orleans. The United States's version of Mardi Gras began in 1856 when six young men formed a Carnival club named Comus, after the Greek god of revelry. The club paraded on Mardi Gras with two small floats followed by maskers, or people wearing detailed costumes, and servants carrying lit torches. People were amazed by the magical scene, and every year since, parades, floats, and masks have been a big part of the celebrations.

The parades and parties that have made Mardi Gras such a famous event in New Orleans are organized and run by societies called krewes.

Secret clubs like Comus are called krewes. Today there are hundreds of krewes in New Orleans, with names often taken from mythology. The Rex krewe (*Rex* means "king" in Latin) was the first to introduce "The King of the Carnival." It is traditional that the king of Rex is the king of the entire Carnival. During Carnival, each krewe gives a ball. Men wear tuxedos, and women wear fancy gowns. A king and a queen are chosen for the ball, and they reign over all the festivities. People stage plays called tableaus, which are usually scenes from history, mythology, or legends.

Each krewe also runs a huge parade with its own theme. The floats are very elaborate, with flowers, streamers, crepe paper, and bright lights. It takes almost an entire year to design and build them. Maskers usually throw the crowd little trinkets such as plastic beads, plastic cups, and coins stamped with the krewe's symbol. One krewe, called Zulu, throws decorated coconuts to the crowd.

One of the parades is run by the Mardi Gras Indians, who have marched in the revelry for more than 100 years. They are Creoles, people of mixed African, Native American, French, and Spanish descent. Their parade has no set route. They dance throughout many neighborhoods in brightly colored costumes decorated with feathers, sequins, rhinestones, and beads. The costumes take months to create and are worn only once. If they meet another group of Mardi Gras Indians on parade, they perform an elaborate dance that includes both African and Native American steps.

King cakes are a popular treat during Carnival. They are large doughnuts decorated with purple, green, and gold icing. Inside the cake is a doll that symbolizes the infant Jesus. If you find the doll, you have to host the next party or buy the next King cake. During this time of year, more than half a million King cakes are eaten.

When the clock strikes midnight on Mardi Gras, the festivities end. It is now the beginning of LENT, and people must be reflective and penitent as they prepare for EASTER. *See* EID AL-FITR.

People dress up in costumes for the parades during Mardi Gras. This man is dressed for Mardi Gras wearing a harlequin mask.

Martin Luther King Jr. Day

People in the United States honor the Reverend Martin Luther King Jr. on the third Monday in January.

King was born in Atlanta, Georgia, on January 15, 1929. At that time, segregation was the law in the South. This meant that blacks had to go to separate schools from whites, eat at separate restaurants, use different restrooms, and drink from separate water fountains. Many people recognized that this separation was not equal and wanted to change things.

For most of his life, King fought for the rights of African Americans. He wanted to end segregation. He gave his most famous speech, entitled "I Have a Dream," in Washington, D.C., on August 28, 1963. Some 250,000 people gathered to hear him and join his fight for equality. His speech told of his vision of an America in which people were judged by their character and not by the color of their skin.

King was awarded the Nobel Peace Prize in 1964 for his work promoting nonviolent methods to win civil rights for African Americans. The next year, he led the fight for voting rights for blacks. He organized a fifty-five-mile march from Selma, Alabama, to Montgomery, the state capital. Some of the marchers were beaten and arrested, but they made their point. In 1965 Congress passed a law that guaranteed millions of African Americans the right to vote.

In 1968 King was planning a strike of sanitation workers in Memphis, Tennessee. On April 4, he stepped out on the balcony of his motel room and was assassinated. People felt strongly that there should be a holiday honoring him. Each year they presented the proposal to Congress, but it failed to pass. On January 15, 1981, more than 100,000 people marched in Washington, D.C., in support of the proposal. Finally in 1983, President Ronald Reagan signed into law a bill making the third Monday in January Martin Luther King Jr. Day.

Many schools and businesses are closed on this day. Students learn about King's life and work. People march in parades and sing songs to honor his beliefs. "I Have a Dream" is broadcast on radio and television.

See HOSTOS DAY.

Martin Luther King Jr. led a number of peaceful protests for equal rights for African Americans.

May Day

May Day is celebrated on May 1 in the United States and Europe. In many countries it is observed as a workers' holiday.

In ancient times, May Day celebrated the coming of spring. Celtic people called their festival Beltane and lit bonfires to honor the sun god. Ancient Romans observed Floralia, or the Festival of Flowers, for one week at the beginning of May. Children decorated pictures and dolls of the goddess Flora with flowers.

These children are dancing around a maypole, which is decorated every year on May Day with streamers and other colorful decorations.

In the past, a popular custom on May Day was the maypole. People usually made the maypole out of a tree branch with its leaves still attached, as a reminder of the coming of spring. They put it up in the village square, where they painted it brightly and decorated it. They hung colorful ribbons and streamers from the top of the pole and danced around it holding the streamers. Sometimes the dancers wore bells and sticks to make noise and frighten away evil spirits. When they leapt high in the air, it was believed to encourage the crops to grow. A May Queen was chosen to commemorate Flora and Maia, the Roman mother goddesses.

In many countries, May Day developed political significance. On May 1, 1886, workers held national strikes in the United States and Canada to fight for an eight-hour workday. In many countries today, May Day is celebrated with parades, political speeches about workers' rights, and fireworks. *See* LABOR DAY.

Memorial Day

Memorial Day is observed on the last Monday in May in the United States and in every country where American soldiers are buried.

It is uncertain exactly when and where the tradition of Memorial Day began. One theory involves a story from Boalsburg, Pennsylvania, where in 1864, the wives and mothers of soldiers killed in the Civil War decorated the graves of their loved ones. Some say that was the first Memorial Day. Waterloo, New York, is thought to have had the first official holiday in 1866. The celebration was called Decoration Day and included a veterans' parade, patriotic speeches, and flags flown at half-staff in memory of soldiers who were killed. By 1869, that custom had become a yearly tradition.

The name was changed to Memorial Day in 1882. Today the holiday commemorates all servicemen and women who have died fighting for the United States. Across the country, flags fly at half-staff, there are parades and speeches, businesses are closed, and gifts are presented to patriotic organizations.

During World War I, poppies became symbols of the lives lost in battle. In the spring, red poppies bloomed on the European battlefields where so many Americans died. Veterans' organizations sell poppies to raise money in aid of disabled veterans and in memory of lives lost.

Special ceremonies are held in different parts of the country. At Gettysburg National Military Park in Pennsylvania, a ceremony marks one of the greatest battles of the Civil War. President Abraham Lincoln's Gettysburg Address is often recited. In Arlington National Cemetery, officials place a wreath on the Tomb of the Unknowns. This monument is the final resting place of unidentified soldiers who were killed in past American wars. In seaside communities, tiny boats filled with flowers are set afloat in honor of people killed at sea. *See* ANZAC DAY.

Although Memorial Day was first observed in the mid-1800s, the federal government did not officially assign the holiday to the last Monday in May until 1968.

Mexican Independence Day

Mexican Independence Day is celebrated in Mexico on September 16.

In the 1500s, Spanish conquistadors invaded Mexico and conquered the Aztecs, the most powerful civilization in Mexico. The Spanish king demanded taxes from the newly conquered people, who were forced to follow Spanish law for the next three hundred years.

Many years later, Father Miguel Hidalgo, a Catholic priest in Mexico City, sought to end Spanish control of Mexico. He believed that the Mexican people should overthrow the Spanish government. On September 16, 1810, he made a powerful speech urging them to fight for their rights. Inspired by his words, the people began to attack government-controlled mines and fortresses. The native Mexicans outnumbered the Spaniards, and soon the natives had won many victories. Unfortunately, the Spanish troops were better armed, and Father Hidalgo was captured and killed in 1811. However, the Mexican people continued the fight. In 1821 Mexico finally won its independence from Spain.

Each year, Mexicans remember Father Hidalgo and celebrate their freedom. They ring church bells and recite his famous speech. The Mexican flag is flown all over the country. It features an eagle eating a snake in the center of a green, white, and red-striped background. The green stands for independence, white for religious freedom, and red for unity. The image comes from an ancient legend that says the Aztecs built their capital, which is now Mexico City, on the spot where they saw an eagle eating a snake. Carnivals and fairs are held in every village and city. People eat traditional Mexican foods such as rice, beans, chicken in mole sauce, sweet potatoes, and burritos. They watch parades and folk dancers. The celebration ends with people setting off firecrackers and watching fireworks displays. *See* CENTRAL AFRICAN REPUBLIC INDEPENDENCE DAY, INDEPENDENCE DAY, *and* PHILIPPINE INDEPENDENCE DAY.

The Column of Independence symbolizes Mexico's fight for independence from Spain.

Mormon Pioneer Day

Mormon Pioneer Day is celebrated on July 24 in Utah and other states with large Mormon populations, such as Idaho, Arizona, Nevada, and Wyoming. The holiday commemorates the day Brigham Young chose the site for the Mormon settlement that later became Salt Lake City, Utah.

In 1839 Joseph Smith founded the Church of Jesus Christ of Latter-day Saints, also known as the Mormon Church. Smith believed that he had found writings of Christian prophets on a mountain in upstate New York that were not included in the Bible. Mormon was one of the prophets Smith discovered. He translated the works and published them as the Book of Mormon.

Smith's church began with only six members, but it grew rapidly. The Latter-day Saints faced persecution for their beliefs because they were straying from the Bible. They were driven away from every place they settled. After being forced out of New York, Ohio, and Missouri, they founded the town of Nauvoo, Illinois. After a mob murdered Smith in Carthage, Illinois, in 1844, many of the Latter-day Saints headed to the desert of the Great Salt Lake valley in what is now Utah with their new leader, Brigham Young. They established themselves in Salt Lake City, which remains their world headquarters. Today membership in the Church of Jesus Christ of Latter-day Saints is close to 10 million.

To observe Mormon Pioneer Day, people reenact the journey to Salt Lake City and hold prayer services. They remember the struggle of the early Mormons to find acceptance and the hardships they suffered as they moved from place to place. *See* HANUKKAH *and* PASSOVER.

In the mid-1800s, Mormons fled religious persecution in Illinois, heading westward in covered wagons like this one, before finally settling near Great Salt Lake in Utah.

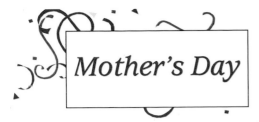

Mother's Day

Mother's Day falls on the second Sunday in May in the United States and England.

The idea of honoring our mothers is extremely old. In ancient Greece, people held celebrations for Rhea, the mother of six important Greek gods and goddesses. In Rome people had festivals for Cybele, the Roman equivalent of Rhea. A similar holiday, called Mothering Sunday, began in England. It fell on the fourth Sunday of LENT. In the seventeenth century, it was customary for people to visit the church of their childhood, where they had been baptized. In addition to visiting the "mother church," people visited their own mothers and often brought a cake or a little gift.

Interest in Mother's Day began in the United States in the nineteenth century. Many people suggested the holiday, but Anna Jarvis is credited with organizing it after her mother's death in 1906. Jarvis greatly appreciated her mother's having given up her own schooling to care for her family. She arranged a memorial service to honor her and asked everyone to wear a white carnation, her mother's favorite flower.

Eventually Jarvis decided that all mothers needed a special day. She organized a committee called the Mother's Day International Association. They wrote letters to the editors of newspapers and spoke with politicians and church leaders about their idea. Jarvis wanted people to remember the sacrifices their mothers made.

West Virginia was the first state to recognize Mother's Day, in 1910. President Woodrow Wilson made it a national holiday in 1914. Children often show their appreciation by serving their mothers breakfast in bed, cleaning house, and making cards. *See* FATHER'S DAY.

Mother's Day is one of the most universally celebrated holidays in the United States. It is the fourth largest card-buying day as well, after CHRISTMAS, VALENTINE'S DAY, and EASTER.

Muhammad's Birthday

Muhammad's Birthday, or Mawlid al-Nabi, is celebrated on the twelfth day of the month of Rabi' I. It is observed throughout the Islamic world.

Mawlid is an Arabic word meaning "birth." Mawlid al-Nabi celebrates the birth of the prophet Muhammad. Muhammad lived in Mecca during the sixth and seventh centuries. It is believed that when he was forty years old, he heard the voice of Allah speaking to him. He began to preach and share Allah's message. His teachings developed into the Islamic religion. The Koran, the holy book of Islam, was given to him by the archangel Gabriel.

The first celebration of Muhammad's birth occurred in 1207 in Upper Mesopotamia, now part of Iraq, Syria, and Turkey. Today each part of the Islamic world has its own traditions and customs. In Lebanon the festival lasts for nine days, with fairs and parades. In Egypt the city of Cairo is lit by thousands of lights. In many areas, special ceremonies occur. One ceremony is the *dhikr,* in which people chant certain words in praise of Allah to a specific rhythm, such as "One true God is great" or "There is no God but Allah."

On Muhammad's birthday people tell the story of his life. These stories are often written in the form of poetry. Two famous poems tell the story of the prophet's cloak. One describes how Muhammad gave the cloak to an outlaw who then repented and joined Islam. In the other, a paralyzed man dreams that the prophet cured him by covering him with the cloak.

Mawlid al-Nabi is also celebrated with feasts. Traditional foods include *tabbouleh* (wheat grain with onions, tomatoes, mint, and parsley) and *djaje mihshi* (roast chicken with rice, spices, and ground lamb). For dessert, people often eat baklava, thin layers of pastry filled with nuts and honey.

Fireworks and gift giving are customary ways to end the festival. *See* CHRISTMAS, CONFUCIUS'S BIRTHDAY, *and* KRISHNA'S BIRTHDAY.

Muhammad, the most revered prophet in Muslim history, studies the Koran.

Native American Indian Powwow

Native American Indian powwows are held in North America year-round. They last three days and are attended by Native Americans and visitors from all over North America

A powwow is a gathering at which tribes celebrate their history, culture, and traditions through dance, song, and visits to family and friends.

Many people believe that gatherings similar to powwows were started by Southern Plains tribes, whose traditions included war dances. They created ceremonies centered around dancing and singing, which were then adopted by tribes across North America.

There are several kinds of powwows. The two most common powwows are the traditional and the competitive. Both powwows honor the culture and spirituality of the tribe through song and dance. At competition powwows, however, dancers also compete for prizes.

Powwows begin with the "Grand Entry"—when the performers come into the area where they will sing and dance. Dancers wear highly decorated traditional outfits. An outfit might feature beadwork, feathers, or braided strips of leather.

The dances tell stories. The men's dance can describe a warrior stalking and capturing an enemy or a hunter defeating a fierce animal. The women's traditional dance requires intense concentration, stamina, and grace. Dancers step in time to the beat of the drum, but they barely lift their feet off the ground.

Boys and girls also participate in dances and competitions. They wear outfits that they and their families decorate.

Powwows help Native American Indians keep their culture and traditions alive. *See* ATI-ATIHAN FESTIVAL *and* WAITANGI DAY.

Native Americans consider powwows to be one of their main cultural events. Powwows take place across North America. This one was held in New Jersey.

Nawruz

See IRANIAN NEW YEAR.

New Year's Day takes place on January 1 in all countries that use the Gregorian calendar.

The celebration of the New Year is one of the oldest holidays that exists. In ancient times, the New Year usually began in the spring. After a long, hard winter, the arrival of warm weather and sunshine seemed like a new beginning. This was also a time when crops were planted and a new harvest cycle began.

When the Romans created a new calendar in the first century B.C., the New Year began in January. The month was named for Janus, the Roman god of all beginnings. Janus had two faces looking in different directions; the Romans believed that one looked back at the past and the other looked to the future. The Romans held huge celebrations to welcome the New Year. They sang, danced, ate, and celebrated all night.

When Christianity spread around the world in the fourth century, these celebrations became more restrained. Dancing and parties were believed to be sinful. Instead people reflected on their lives and asked God to forgive their sins. But by the Middle Ages (A.D. 500–1500), people were celebrating once again. New Year's Day became a festive holiday. At that time, it was traditional to give gifts. It is said that in the late 1500s, Queen Elizabeth I of England received so many gifts from her subjects that she did not have enough room to keep them all.

New Year's Day is celebrated all over the world. This New Year's ceremony was held in Thailand.

Today the countdown to the New Year begins on New Year's Eve. People gather with friends and family that evening and have parties. In Times Square in New York City, a huge lit New Year's Eve Ball is lowered down a pole as crowds of people count the final seconds of the old year. At midnight everyone cheers and makes a lot of noise. Centuries ago people believed that loud noises scared away evil spirits, so they rang bells, set off firecrackers, and banged drums when the New Year began.

At midnight, people also sing a Scottish song, "Auld Lang Syne." The title means "old long ago," and it celebrates the good old days. This custom began in Britain in the eighteenth century when New Year's Eve parties ended with the singing of this song. The lyrics were written in 1788 by Robert Burns, a Scottish poet.

There are different New Year's traditions around the world. In Denmark the New Year begins with loud explosions. Young people throw old crockery against friends' and neighbors' doors. People in Iceland clean up trash on New Year's Eve and perform elf dances. Elves were once believed to come out that night, and the dance is to welcome them. In Ecuador families build scarecrows and write lists of everyone's faults. At midnight they dance around the scarecrow and read the lists. Then they set fire to the scarecrow and the lists—as they go up in flames, so do the participants' faults. Everyone starts the New Year with a clean slate.

Many cultures hold that the new year brings a fresh start. The Chinese and Japanese pay all their debts. In Madagascar, people pour water on their heads to wash away their sins. In many parts of the world, people clean their homes and buy new clothes to start the New Year fresh. Some people make New Year's resolutions to improve themselves in the year ahead. In Belgium children decorate a list of future good deeds with ribbons and bows and give it to their parents.

Visiting friends and family is a tradition on New Year's Day. In some countries, it is believed that the first person who visits will set the tone for the rest of the year. In Scotland and England, this custom is called first-footing.

Some people believe that the first food one eats in the New Year can also bring luck. In Pennsylvania Dutch country, people eat sauerkraut. In the southern United States, they believe black-eyed peas and rice give good luck. In France, people traditionally eat pancakes. *See* CHINESE NEW YEAR, KOREAN NEW YEAR, *and* VIETNAMESE NEW YEAR.

Hundreds of thousands of people gather in Times Square in New York City to celebrate New Year's Eve with fireworks, party favors, and the famous New Year's Eve Ball, which is lowered in the last sixty seconds of the old year.

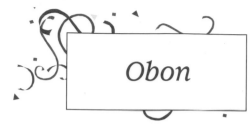

Obon

Obon, also called Urabon, is celebrated by Japanese Buddhists around the world from July 13 to15 or August 13 to 15.

Obon is a festival for the dead. Buddhists believe that the spirits of the deceased visit the earth at this time. The Buddhist service is based upon the legend of Maudgalyayana, a disciple of Buddha. After Maudgalyayana's mother died, he used his special abilities to see how she was doing in her afterlife. He thought she looked thin and hungry. Maudgalyayana gave her a bowl of rice, but when she tried to eat it, the rice turned to fire. Maudgalyayana asked Buddha what to do. Buddha advised him to give food to his fellow monks on the fifteenth day of the seventh month. In return, he was to ask the monks to perform a memorial service for his mother. Maudgalyayana did this, and as a result, his mother was saved from the realm of the hungry ghosts.

Today Obon is held to save all spirits from the realm of hungry ghosts. Throughout the three days of the celebration, the spirits are spoken to as if they were alive and are given food at each meal, including potatoes cooked with sesame seeds, fruits, cakes, and sweets.

Traditional Buddhist dances, called *bon-odori,* are performed on the last day of the celebration. Dancers move in a circle to the beat of the *taiko* drum. Centuries ago, the *taiko* was used to summon people to the temple. Now it is placed on a high tower representing the watchtowers used years ago in Japanese villages. The dancers wear traditional kimonos. Some people wear a *yujkata,* a thin cotton garment that is shorter than a kimono and more comfortable in the summer. The dances, which consist of four or five repeated movements, often tell traditional stories and legends. Sometimes the dancers perform with *kachi-kachi,* pieces of bamboo that they click together to the beat of the *taiko. See* ALL SOULS' DAY *and* DAY OF THE DEAD.

Monks pray to the dead at a shrine during the festival of Obon.

Orange Day

Orange Day, also known as Orangemen's Day, is celebrated on July 12 by Protestants in Northern Ireland.

Orange Day commemorates the Battle of the Boyne, which took place in 1690. The trouble began two years earlier, when King James II tried to reintroduce Catholicism to England. The English Parliament disapproved, so it asked William of Orange, a Protestant, to replace James II on the throne. James fled to Ireland. Each side raised powerful armies of about 30,000 men, and they fought at the Boyne River. The Protestants won the battle. The celebration of Orange Day recalls this early fight in what is now a centuries-old dispute. Irish Catholics formed underground societies that worked to restore the throne to James's line. In re-

These Orangemen are marching in an Orange Day parade. They belong to the Orange Order, the Protestant organization that seeks to keep Protestants in power in Northern Ireland.

sponse, the Protestants formed the Orange Order, committed to maintaining relations with Protestant England.

Today Orange Day is celebrated with parades. Protestant men wear bowler hats and orange ribbons as they march through the streets. Some Protestants use the day to express their desire for Northern Ireland (separated from the Catholic south since 1920) to remain part of the United Kingdom. In previous years, the Orangemen marched through Catholic areas. However, due to many bloody conflicts, that does not occur as often. Towns and villages also decorate their streets with banners, flags, and symbols of the Orange Order. *See* JOAN OF ARC, FEAST OF.

Our Lady of Fatima Day

Our Lady of Fatima Day is celebrated in Portugal on July 13.

On May 13, 1917, three children from the village of Fatima—Lucinda, Jacinto, and Francisca dos Santos—said that the Virgin Mary, the mother of Jesus, had appeared before them. At first, no one believed the children. But on the thirteenth day of every month, the same event occurred. Soon adults followed the children to see the miraculous vision.

Five months later, on October 13, about 70,000 people were present when the vision appeared for the last time. It is reported that she said she was the "Lady of the Rosary" and asked the gathered people to pray the rosary every day. She also wanted a church to be built in her honor in Fatima. Believers make pilgrimages to the church on the thirteenth day of every month. The biggest pilgrimages occur on May 13 and October 13. Our Lady of Fatima Day is observed on July 13 because on that day a group of adults saw the Virgin Mary for the first time. *See* CHRISTMAS *and* ASSUMPTION DAY.

The Rosary

The rosary is a string of beads with a crucifix attached. The beads are divided into five sections, and may be made of wood, metal, plastic, or other materials.

Catholics use the rosary to count a series of prayers (also called the rosary). The prayers include the following: the Apostles' Creed, Our Father, Hail Mary, and Glory Be. The series starts and ends at the crucifix. As they make their way through the rosary, Catholics say one prayer while holding each bead.

Ever since the Virgin Mary reportedly appeared in the town of Fatima, millions of people have made pilgrimages to the Basilica of Our Lady of Fatima, the church that was built at the site of the visions.

Palm Sunday

Palm Sunday is celebrated one week before EASTER by Christians throughout the world. The date of Easter is determined by the phases of the moon, so the date of Palm Sunday changes each year.

Palm Sunday commemorates the day that Jesus rode into Jerusalem. According to his apostles, people waved palm leaves to greet him. In churches on this day, palm leaves are blessed and given to the congregation. The inside of the church is often decorated with palms. The church saves the palms that are blessed, which are later burned to make the ashes used on ASH WEDNESDAY the following year.

Different customs are observed in various parts of the world. In Rome the pope is carried in a special chair on the shoulders of eight men as he blesses the palms. In Mexico villagers decorate large crosses with fruit. In many places, the church is given a special cleaning. It is believed that if the dirt swept from the church floor is spread on the crops, it will bring a good harvest. *See* SUKKOT.

Pan-American Day

Pan-American Day is held on April 14 in North, Central, and South America.

The holiday honors the founding of the Commercial Bureau of American Republics on April 14, 1889, in Washington, D.C., at the first Pan-American Conference attended by the United States. The organization was created to discuss national and international problems, settle disputes, and promote greater understanding among countries. Its goal is to strengthen peace and security by building relationships among the various countries of the Americas.

The Pan-American Plaza in Indianapolis, Indiana, is a tribute, like the one in Washington, D.C., to efforts at international understanding.

Each member country has its own celebration, but the largest is held at the Pan-American Union building in Washington, D.C. Flags from every member country are displayed, and people perform native songs and dances. Students from all over the Americas travel to Washington, where they learn about other cultures and study world policies. *See* EARTH DAY.

Passover

Passover, or *pesach,* is celebrated from the fifteenth to the twenty-first day of the Jewish month Nisan. It usually occurs between March 27 and April 24 and is celebrated by Jewish people all over the world.

Passover is an eight-day celebration that rejoices in the freedom of Jews from slavery. More than three thousand years ago, the Jews settled in Egypt. At first they lived peacefully with the Egyptians. But when the pharaoh (the king of Egypt) decided to build magnificent new cities, he enslaved all the Jews. For many years they worked under horrible conditions. When they asked God to help them, God told one of them, Moses, to lead the Jewish people out of Egypt. Moses demanded that the pharaoh set the Jewish slaves free. However, the pharaoh did not believe that Moses had God's support, and he refused. God sent many plagues to Egypt to convince the pharaoh of his power—swarms of locusts that destroyed crops, hailstorms, and diseases. Still the pharaoh would not let the Jewish people go.

Finally God decided to kill the firstborn son of every Egyptian. He warned Moses of his plan, and Moses instructed the Jewish people to sacrifice lambs and smear the blood around their doorways. In that way, when the angel of death passed by, it would know not to take anyone from that household. That night, the pharaoh lost his eldest son. He was so sad that he let Moses lead the Jewish people out of Egypt. The people left in such a hurry that they did not have time to prepare. They quickly made dough out of flour and water and carried it with them. Out in the desert, they baked the dough on stones and made unleavened bread. Unleavened bread is flat because it has no yeast in it to make it rise.

The pharaoh's sorrow turned to anger, and he ordered his soldiers to go after the Jewish people. The soldiers caught up to them on the banks of the Red Sea and trapped them there. Once again, God helped

There is always a plate on the table at Passover that holds the holiday's major symbols: greens, an egg, a lamb bone, bitter herbs, and a sweet dish called haroset.

by parting the waters of the Red Sea. The people safely crossed to the other side, but when the Egyptians tried to follow, the waters closed in on them and the soldiers drowned. The Jewish people were finally free.

Today Jewish families remember the passing of the angel of death and celebrate the journey through the desert to freedom. The holiday begins with a *seder,* a feast at which they eat special foods that symbolize their struggles. The story of the exodus, or journey, is read from a book called the *Haggadah.* The seder begins when the youngest child present asks, "Why does this night differ from all other nights?" The child also asks, "Why do we eat only bitter herbs? Why is food dipped in salt water?" The stories in the *Haggadah* answer these questions and tell the meaning of each symbol.

Each food has a special meaning. Greens symbolize the coming of spring.

The story of the Jews' flight from Egypt comes from the book of Exodus in the Torah, but the story is read at Passover from a book called the Haggadah.

Hard-boiled eggs stand for the spiritual strength of Jewish people and remind them of the new beginning when the Jews left Egypt. A lamb bone reminds people of the lambs that were sacrificed for their blood so the angel of death would recognize Jewish households. Bitter herbs are eaten as a symbol of the hardships endured by the Jewish people during their slavery in Egypt. *Haroset,* a mixture of wine, apples, nuts, sugar, and cinnamon, represents the clay used by the Jewish slaves to make bricks for the pharaoh's cities and the pyramids.

During the eight days of Passover, people eat only unleavened bread called *matzo,* symbolic of the bread the Jews ate in the desert. At the *seder,* a special cloth is laid on the table, and three pieces of matzo are placed on it. A piece is broken off the middle matzo and hidden. At the end of the meal, children look for the missing piece, called the *afikomen.* When they find it, they are rewarded with gifts. Then the piece is broken into many parts and distributed to everyone as the last taste of the *seder.* A glass of wine is also poured for the prophet Elijah. According to Jewish belief, Elijah will appear during Passover before the coming of the Messiah. Children watch this glass carefully to see if he has arrived and taken a sip. *See* EASTER.

Pearl Harbor Day

Pearl Harbor Day is observed on December 7 in the United States. Pearl Harbor is in Hawaii, about six miles west of Honolulu. It is the site of a naval base and the headquarters of the U.S. Pacific Fleet.

On December 7, 1941, during World War II, Japanese airplanes and submarines attacked Pearl Harbor. The United States had not yet entered the war, but relations were strained with Japan because of Japan's alliance with Germany and Italy. The attack was severe. About 3,000 American servicemen and civilians were killed. The next day, the United States declared war on Japan and entered World War II.

On Pearl Harbor Day, people remember those who were killed in the attack and the American entrance into World War II. Speeches are given by politicians and military personnel, and parades are held. Memorial services are held at war monuments. A marble memorial was built over the spot where a sunken battleship, the U.S.S. *Arizona,* lies on the bottom of the harbor. Memorial services are also held for the families of the civilians who were killed. *See* ANZAC DAY *and* MEMORIAL DAY.

A memorial marks the spot where a U.S. ship sank in Pearl Harbor.

Pentecost

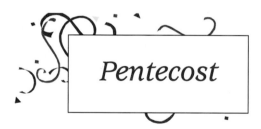

Pentecost is celebrated by Christians worldwide on the seventh Sunday after EASTER.

On this day, the apostles celebrated the Jewish holiday Shavuot. The Bible says that as the apostles prayed, the Holy Spirit gave them the ability to speak many languages. They began to preach about Jesus Christ to thousands of people. During Shavuot, more than 3,000 people were baptized into the Christian church. As a result, Pentecost is considered the beginning of Christianity. Symbols of the holiday include the red rose, which represents the fire that gave the apostles the ability to speak many languages. The dove symbolizes the Holy Spirit. In Germany and Austria, it is common to hang a painted dove above the altar in the church.

In England the holy day is called Whitsunday, or White Sunday, for the white garments worn by the newly baptized. Centuries ago it was one of two days during the year when people could be baptized.

Pentecost is traditionally associated with the arrival of spring. One custom is to gather green branches in the woods to decorate a person in the village, who is known as Green George, or the Leaf Man. Children try to find the Leaf Man in a game called hunting the green man. *See* ST. JOHN THE BAPTIST DAY.

Philippine Independence Day

José Rizal founded the Philippine League in hopes of gaining independence peacefully. He was executed in 1896.

Philippine Independence Day is celebrated on June 12 in the Philippine Islands.

In 1521 the explorer Ferdinand Magellan claimed these islands for Spain. Other Spanish explorers followed. They named the islands "Islas Filipinas" in honor of King Philip II. For more than 300 years, Spain ruled the Philippines. The Spanish owned most of the land, and they made the Filipino people pay taxes, even though the Filipinos had no voice in the government.

Throughout the years of Spanish rule, the Filipinos protested their lack of rights, but Spanish troops were always able to stop the uprisings. On July 3, 1892, José Rizal founded the Philippine League to fight for independence. The Spanish considered the league dangerous and had Rizal deported and later executed.

Rizal's death angered the people, and they staged a serious revolt. For a number of reasons, the United States and Spain went to war in 1898. The Filipinos hoped the United States would help them win their fight, and on June 12, 1898, the Filipinos declared themselves independent. On January 23, 1899, the Philippine Constitution was ratified. The Philippines was the first Asian country to have a constitutional democracy. However, the United States controlled the Philippines for many years, finally granting independence in 1946.

The Filipinos celebrate their long-delayed independence with parades, exhibits, cultural shows, trade fairs, and fireworks displays. There are tributes to the leaders at various monuments and museums. *See* CENTRAL AFRICAN REPUBLIC INDEPENDENCE DAY, INDEPENDENCE DAY, MEXICAN INDEPENDENCE DAY, *and* TEXAS INDEPENDENCE DAY.

Polish Constitution Day

Polish Constitution Day is celebrated on May 3, commemorating the day in 1791 on which the first constitution of Poland was adopted.

In the 1700s, Poland was a monarchy, but the king was elected by the nobles, so the nobles had more power than the king. The common people had no voice in government. The ideas of liberty expressed in the American Revolution in the 1770s and the French Revolution in 1789 carried over into Poland. On May 3, 1791, the Polish people created a new constitution that gave more people the right to vote, guaranteed certain freedoms, and changed some rules of government. One important change was the end of the *liberum* veto, under which any noble could prevent the passage of a law simply by saying, "I disapprove." This system had made the Polish government weak.

Russia, Prussia, and Austria wanted the Polish government to stay weak so they could take Polish land. The tsar (emperor) of Russia ordered that the new constitution be given up. The Polish people refused, so Russia invaded and took over much of the kingdom of Poland. Tadeusz Kosciuszko, a military man who had helped the Americans win independence from Britain, led a revolution against the new Russian rulers. Although they fought bravely, the Polish people lost the battle, and the rest of Poland was divided among Russia, Prussia, and Austria. The country practically disappeared from maps until 1918, when the pieces were put back together following World War I. The re-created country was unstable. The people were poor, and most cities had been destroyed in the war. Poland suffered horribly again twenty years later, in World War II. The years since then have been spent rebuilding the country in the midst of rapid political and economic changes.

On Polish Constitution Day, people give thanks for the freedoms they enjoy today. They celebrate with parades and community gatherings. People wear regional costumes and play festive music such as polkas. They eat Polish foods, such as pierogi (dough stuffed with meat, potato, or cheese), *naleszniki* (thin pancakes with various fillings), and *paczki* (jelly doughnuts rolled in sugar). *See* BASTILLE DAY, CITIZENSHIP DAY, *and* REPUBLIC DAY.

This painting shows Poles revolting against Russian troops in Warsaw in 1830.

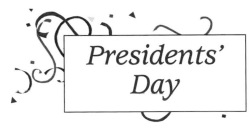

Presidents' Day

Presidents' Day is observed on the third Monday in February in the United States. All former U.S. presidents are honored on this day. The holiday originally honored George Washington and Abraham Lincoln. For many years, separate holidays marked each president's birthday in February. Because the days were so close together, they were made into one holiday.

George Washington is considered the father of the United States. He led the Continental army during the Revolutionary War. In October 1781, he won the Battle of Yorktown, which led to the end of the war. After gaining its independence, the United States developed a new government. Washington helped create the Constitution that has shaped all the laws of the country. He was elected the first president and served two terms.

Abraham Lincoln was elected to the House of Representatives from Illinois in 1846. In 1860, he was elected president. Many people in the South did not want a president who was against slavery, as Lincoln was. Some southern states left the Union and formed their own country, the Confederate States of America. The Civil War began when Confederate troops attacked Union soldiers. Lincoln wanted to keep the United States together, so he reluctantly fought the bitter war for four years. In 1865, the Confederates surrendered. Five days later, Lincoln was watching a play with his wife at Ford's Theater when an actor named John Wilkes Booth shot him. He died the next morning.

Americans have honored these two great men in many ways. The country's capital is named for Washington, and fifty-five counties are named for either Washington or Lincoln. Washington's portrait is on the dollar bill and the quarter, and Lincoln's is on the five-dollar bill and the penny. Both presidents have monuments dedicated to them in Washington, D.C. Both men are also depicted on Mount Rushmore. On Presidents' Day, government offices, businesses, and schools are closed. Wreaths are placed on all of the presidents' grave sites. *See* EMANCIPATION DAY *and* INDEPENDENCE DAY.

Likenesses of Presidents George Washington, Thomas Jefferson, Theodore Roosevelt, and Abraham Lincoln are carved into Mount Rushmore in South Dakota. The monument took fourteen years to complete and stands higher than the pyramids in Egypt.

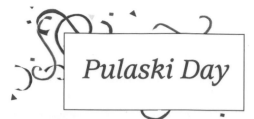

Pulaski Day

Pulaski Day is observed on October 11 in most of the United States. The day honors Count Casimir Pulaski, a hero of the Revolutionary War. As a young man in Poland, he led a revolt against Russia, which controlled part of his country. The revolt failed, and Pulaski was forced to flee. He went to Paris, where he met Benjamin Franklin, a representative of the American states fighting for their Independence from Britain. Franklin persuaded Pulaski to join the fight. Pulaski was a skilled fighter, but he had problems with American troops. He spoke no English and refused to take orders. In 1778 he resigned from the army and established an independent corps called the Pulaski Legion. He was wounded in a battle to free Savannah, Georgia, from British control and died on October 11, 1779.

The celebration of Pulaski Day is most popular in communities with large Polish-American populations. It is observed with patriotic parades and military exercises. In New York City, more than 100,000 people march down Fifth Avenue on Pulaski Day. *See* INDEPENDENCE DAY.

After leaving Poland in the 1770s, Count Pulaski earned fame in the Revolutionary War as George Washington's aide-de-camp at the Battle of the Brandywine in Pennsylvania. An expert cavalryman, he organized a cavalry corps that became known as the Pulaski Legion.

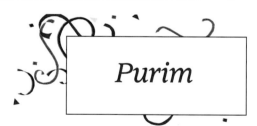

Purim

Purim, the Feast of Lots, is a religious holiday held on the fourteenth day of Adar (February–March) on the Jewish calendar. It is celebrated by Jewish people all over the world.

The holiday celebrates the story of Esther as told in the Hebrew Scriptures. Purim honors Esther's bravery in saving the Jewish people from the Persian prime minister Haman, who hoped to see them killed. The lots refer to numbered sticks; Haman drew one to see on what day the Jews would be executed. On this day, the Book of Esther is read in synagogues, and people make noise and hiss whenever Haman's name is read. Children wear costumes and act out the story.

Purim is also a time to give to the poor, since the first Purim festival was held for both the rich and the poor. People give gifts called *shalachmanot,* usually candy, fruit, or nuts. A favorite food is *hamantaschen,* little cookies filled with prunes or poppy seeds and said to resemble Haman's hat or pocket. *See* SUKKOT.

80

Raksha Bandhama

Raksha Bandhama, or Brother and Sister Day, is celebrated throughout India during the Hindu month of Sravana (July–August).

It is an ancient holiday when the bonds between brother and sister are strengthened and reaffirmed. As a signal of the special relationship between the siblings, girls tie *rakhis* on their brothers' wrists. *Rakhis* are bracelets made of cotton or silk thread. Typically they are very colorful and sometimes gold or silver. They are meant to protect the brother and guard him from evil. In some places, the sister also places vermilion (bright red) paste on the brother's forehead or puts barley sprigs behind his ears to ward off bad luck.

People wear bright, colorful clothing when they go to the market on Raksha Bandhama. Traditionally married women wear saris—a single piece of cloth wrapped around the body and worn with a blouse. Unmarried women and young girls wear long flowing trousers called shalwar *and a blouse called a* kameez.

In return, brothers give gifts of clothing or jewelry to their sisters. They are expected to protect and help the sisters who gave them the *rakhis*. According to legend, when the god Indra received a bracelet from his wife, Indrani, he was able to defeat the demons he fought against.

To celebrate Raksha Bandhama, family members go to the market early in the day to buy the *rakhis* and gifts. They wear their best and brightest clothes. If a family has only girls or only boys, they ask a friend or relative to act as a brother or sister during the festival. It is a great honor to be chosen as brother by a girl.

In Nepal, the Brahmins, the highest division of Nepalese society, chant as they tie golden threads around one anothers' wrists to give the thread the power to protect its owner. They also change the *janai*, threads that all Brahmin wear around their necks. The necklace is made of three strings that represent the three main Hindu gods, Brahma, Vishnu, and Shiva. *See* CHILDREN'S DAY.

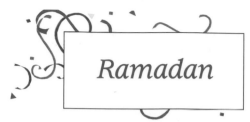

Ramadan

Ramadan is the ninth month of the Islamic lunar calendar. The lunar year has 354 days, making it ten or eleven days shorter than the solar year on which the Western calendar is based. This means that Ramadan moves from year to year. Some years it occurs in winter, and others in summer.

The celebration honors the day when the Koran, the holy book of Islam, was given to the prophet Muhammad by the archangel Gabriel. After receiving the vision, Muhammad preached in the city of Mecca that there was only one God. Many people did not like this idea, and they forced him to flee from Mecca. He and his followers went to Medina and formed an army, which slowly became stronger and more powerful. In A.D. 630 they marched back to Mecca and were able to spread the religion of Islam. Two important victories, the Battle of Badr and the conquest of Mecca, are also remembered during Ramadan.

Ramadan begins the instant the new moon is seen in the night sky following sunset on the first day of the month. In many places, the first sight of the moon is announced by gunfire or a cannon shot.

Ramadan is a time of fasting. During the entire month, no one eats any food or drinks any water from sunrise to sunset. Some Muslims even try to avoid swallowing too much of their saliva. Tradition says that as soon as it is light enough to distinguish between a white thread and a black one, the fast begins. Children begin to participate when they are twelve years old. Only the elderly, the ill, or mothers with babies are not required to fast.

People fast to teach themselves self-discipline and to defeat Satan. It is believed that all sins will be forgiven if the fast is faithfully followed. Muslim leaders say that fasting puts people in a fresh state of mind, helps them appreciate the suffering of the less

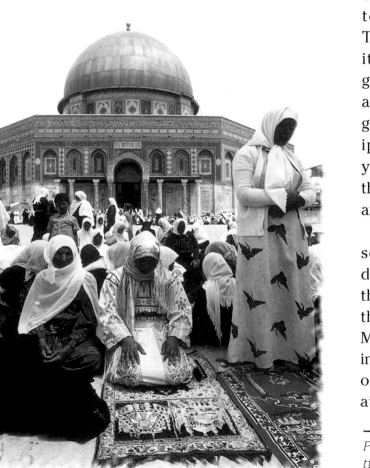

People gather to pray several times a day during Ramadan.

fortunate, and teaches patience. However, five acts can destroy the good done by fasting: slander, lying, talking ill of someone behind his or her back, a false promise, and greed. During Ramadan people must also avoid kissing, smoking, bathing, and receiving injections.

During Ramadan, dates and water is the preferred snack to break the daily fast. At the end of Ramadan, people are able to eat food like this at the festival of Eid al-Fitr.

During the day, Muslims spend a lot of time praying, reading, or sleeping. Restaurants are closed, and there is little activity in the streets. The people go to mosques to pray. A mosque is a large open room covered with carpets. There is no furniture and no pictures on the walls to distract worshipers from thoughts of Allah, the Islamic God. Before entering the mosque, worshipers remove their shoes and wash their hands, faces, and feet. People use the time during Ramadan to read the entire Koran—114 chapters, called *suras,* and more than 6,000 verses.

The Ramadan breakfast occurs at sunset. It is called *suhur.* When Ramadan occurs during the winter, the days are short so the meal is light. If it occurs during the long days of summer, the meal is much larger because it will be many hours before people can eat again.

At dusk people listen for a call telling them the sun has set. The signal comes from the minaret, a tower on the mosque from which people are called to prayer. To break the fast, people drink water, eat a few dates, and then pray together. After prayers, families gather for a meal called *iftar.* Mosques serve *iftar* for people who cannot afford to buy food for themselves or their families.

The holiday ends on the first day of the next month, Shawwal. To celebrate, Muslims hold a three-day festival called EID AL-FITR. They say to each other, "*Eid Mubarak,*" which means "blessed festival." They spend much of Ramadan preparing for the festival, sending cards and buying presents for family and friends. Muslims give to the poor all year, but they are especially generous during Ramadan. They give money to poor families a few days before Eid al-Fitr starts so those families can buy food. *See* LENT *and* YOM KIPPUR.

Republic Day

Republic Day is celebrated on October 29 in Turkey. The holiday commemorates the founding of the Turkish Republic in 1923 and the election of Mustafa Kemal Atatürk as the first president.

After World War I, the Ottoman Empire was in ruins. Turkey was at the political center of the empire, but rather than continue as the most powerful group in a weak empire, many Turks fought to set up an independent country. Mustafa Kemal led the fight for independence and was later named Atatürk, which means "father of the Turks." He became the first president of Turkey on October 29, 1923. The celebration of Republic Day lasts for two days. Large parades are held in which marchers wear traditional clothing and play Turkish music. There are also torchlight processions, dancing, theatrical presentations, and fireworks. *See* POLISH CONSTITUTION DAY *and* BASTILLE DAY.

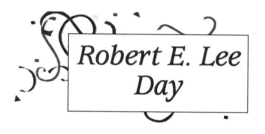

Robert E. Lee Day

Robert E. Lee Day is observed on the third Monday in January in the states of Alabama, Arkansas, Florida, Georgia, Kentucky, Louisiana, Mississippi, North Carolina, South Carolina, Tennessee, and Virginia.

Robert E. Lee was a general in charge of much of the southern army during the Civil War. The troops under his leadership were the most successful of the southern, or Confederate, troops. In 1865 Lee was given supreme command of all Confederate troops. By that time, however, the southern troops were weak. They held their ground for a while, but the Union, or Northern, soldiers were too strong. Lee surrendered at Appomattox Court House in 1865, a move that ended the Civil War. After the war, Lee became president of Washington College, which was later renamed Washington and Lee University in Lexington, Virginia. He died in 1870 at his home at Washington College.

People in the South celebrate Lee's important role in history with parades and picnics in his honor. In some places there are reenactments of his major battles. *See* EMANCIPATION DAY.

Although Robert E. Lee (on the right) opposed secession, he fought against the North to defend his home state of Virginia. Because of his role in the Civil War, his U.S. citizenship was revoked. It was not restored until 1970.

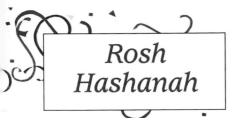

Rosh Hashanah

Jewish communities around the world celebrate Rosh Hashanah on the first and second days of Tishri, the first month of the Jewish calendar (between September 6 and October 4). Rosh Hashanah is the beginning of the Jewish year.

Rosh Hashanah is one of two Jewish High Holy Days. YOM KIPPUR is the other. The High Holy Days are a time when people reflect on their lives and try to change for the better.

There are three groups of prayers that take place on Rosh Hashanah. The first reminds people that God rules the world; the second says that God hears the blowing of the shofar *and will respond; and the third says that God does not forget people's deeds.*

Rosh Hashanah is also known as Yom ha-Din, or Day of Judgment. It is believed to be the day that God writes names in the Book of Life for the coming year. The Book of Life has three sections: one for the wicked, one for the good, and one for those who fall in between. Where a person's name appears in the book indicates the type of fortune he or she will have in the next year. Those who have done wrong can repent and seek forgiveness during the ten days between Rosh Hashanah and Yom Kippur. This may reverse the judgment against them before the Book of Life is sealed.

Rosh Hashanah begins at sundown with a family meal. The table is set with a white cloth. White is the color of innocence, newness, and purity. Two candles are lit and the *She-Heheyanu,* the prayer of thanksgiving, is said. A cup of sweet wine is poured, and a blessing is given for the holiday and for the meal. Challah, a sweet bread, is served. Another tradition is to cut an apple into pieces and dip the pieces in honey. People pray that the New Year will be as sweet as the challah, apples, and honey.

On the next day, people go to synagogue. Prayers are said from the *mahzor,* the High Holy Day prayer book. The *shofar,* or ram's horn, is blown many times during the service. The person chosen to blow the horn is called the *toké aa'ba-shofar,* which is Hebrew for the "shofar blower." The shofar blower is a man of singular piety and purity of conduct.

After the service, Orthodox Jews go to a nearby stream or the ocean and observe the custom of *tashlikh.* Having filled their pockets with crumbs to symbolize the sins of the past year, they throw the crumbs into the water so their sins will be carried away. *See* ASH WEDNESDAY.

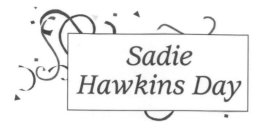

Sadie Hawkins Day

Sadie Hawkins Day is celebrated on the first Saturday in November in the United States.

Sadie Hawkins is a character from the comic strip "L'il Abner," created by Al Capp. She is a spinster who keeps hoping that she will find a man to marry. Capp invented her holiday as a time when unmarried women can chase bachelors. If the man is caught, it is believed that he must marry his pursuer. Sadie Hawkins Day is celebrated by schools with dances to which the girls must invite the boys.

A similar custom used to occur on LEAP YEAR DAY, when women could ask men to marry them. If the men refused, they had to pay a fee. Leap Year Day is sometimes called Ladies' Day or Bachelors' Day. *See* APRIL FOOLS' DAY.

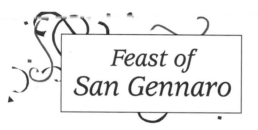

Feast of San Gennaro

The Feast of San Gennaro is celebrated on September 19 in Italy and by Italian communities around the world.

San Gennaro, also known as St. Januarius, served as bishop of Benevento in Italy 1,700 years ago. According to legend, he suffered great hardship because of his religious beliefs. He was thrown into a fiery furnace and left in a den of wild animals. No matter how much torture he was put through, however, San Gennaro survived and remained faithful to his God. Eventually he was ordered to be put to death by decapitation. His body and a vial of his blood were taken to Naples.

Each year on September 19, the anniversary of his death, a strange and mysterious thing is said to happen: The congealed blood in the vial becomes liquid. This event, which many people believe is a miracle, draws huge crowds to worship and rejoice in Naples. Little Italy in New York City holds a festival. People parade down Mulberry Street carrying a bust of San Gennaro and create shrines on the streets. The fair lasts for several days. *See* OUR LADY OF FATIMA DAY.

This statue is displayed at the San Gennaro Festival in New York City's Little Italy. People leave gifts of money at the statue's base.

Sechseläuten

Sechseläuten, a two-day celebration of the start of spring, is held in Zurich, Switzerland, beginning on the third Sunday in April.

The festival begins with a children's parade on Sunday. Children wear historical costumes and carry the Boogg, a snowman that symbolizes winter. The Boogg, made of cloth and stuffed with cotton, contains firecrackers.

Young girls wear traditional clothing during the springtime festival of Sechseläuten in Zurich, Switzerland.

That evening at six o'clock, someone rings the city's bells. During the winter months, bells are normally rung at seven. The hour's difference on Sechseläuten signals the beginning of spring. According to a custom that began in the fourteenth century, the workday ends an hour early during spring and summer.

On Monday people gather at Lake Zurich when the bells ring again at six o'clock. People on horseback gallop around the Boogg while bands play hunting marches. Then the snowman is set on fire and the firecrackers explode. At night the festivities continue with torchlight parades and feasts. *See* MAY DAY.

St. John the Baptist Day

St. John the Baptist Day is celebrated on June 24, the date of his birth, in Christian communities around the world.

John was the cousin of Jesus. Christians believe he was chosen to prepare the way for Jesus. Throughout his life, John preached about Jesus and urged people to repent for their sins. He baptized many people, including Jesus himself.

French Canadians celebrate St. John the Baptist Day with a large festival. They hold street fairs and parades with dancing and music. The streets are decorated with flowers and images of St. John. In Mexico this day is a major holiday, called Día de San Juan. St. John is the patron saint of water. People decorate fountains and wells, and it is traditional to bathe in streams and rivers. Bands play, and people throw flowers to the bathers. In cities the celebration takes place at pools or bathhouses with swimming and diving contests. Small mules made out of corn husks, decorated with flowers and filled with candy, are popular gifts. *See* PENTECOST.

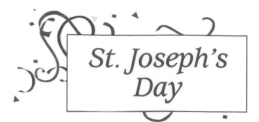

St. Joseph's Day

St. Joseph's Day is celebrated on March 19 by Christians in Western Europe, North America, and South America, and on July 29 in southern Asia, the Middle East, and the eastern Mediterranean. It is especially popular in Italy and with Sicilian Catholics living in the United States.

Joseph was the foster father of Jesus. As a carpenter in Nazareth, he provided for Mary and Jesus. He has become the patron saint of many groups, including the poor, carpenters, and laborers. In Italy the feast is considered FATHER'S DAY and honors all fathers.

It is believed that the feast began one year in Sicily when there was a drought. The people prayed to Joseph, their patron saint, to help them. They promised to hold a huge festival in his honor if it rained. The rains came, and the day has been celebrated ever since.

St. Joseph's Day is a time of generosity. Communities prepare a "table of St. Joseph," and food, drinks, flowers, and candles are donated to place on the table. Three guests representing Jesus, Mary, and Joseph have places of honor at the table, and poor people, widows, and orphans are invited to eat with them. The food is blessed by a priest and by a child who represents Jesus.

Traditional foods include bread shaped like the beard of St. Joseph and a special soup made by combining random ingredients brought by participants. Fish is also served, probably because the celebration falls during LENT, when Christians are supposed to avoid eating meat. The fish is also a symbol of Christ because the five letters in the Greek word for fish (ichthus) are an acronym of "Jesus Christ, Son of God, Savior." The fish also symbolizes baptism. *See* ASSUMPTION DAY.

St. Joseph's staff burst into a flowery bloom when he learned that he had been chosen to be Mary's husband.

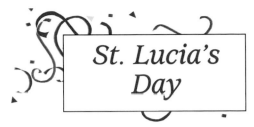

St. Lucia's Day

St. Lucia's Day is celebrated on December 13 in Sweden, Denmark, Finland, Norway, and by Scandinavian communities in the United States.

Legend says that St. Lucia was a beautiful girl who lived in Sicily in the third century. Her beauty attracted a wealthy nobleman who wanted to marry her. She opposed the marriage because the nobleman did not believe in God. To end his desire, Lucia cut out her eyes and gave all her money to the poor. As a reward for her strong faith, God restored her sight. Later in life, she was stabbed to death in the neck with a sword. Because of her hardships, St. Lucia is the patron saint of blindness and the saint who protects against throat infections.

The name Lucia means "light." It is believed that she blinded herself on the winter solstice, the shortest day of the year. After the winter solstice (December 20, 21, or 22), the days grow longer. Bonfires became a tradition on St. Lucia's Day to celebrate the lengthening days. Many people also keep candles burning all night in their homes.

In Sweden St. Lucia's Day also marks the beginning of the CHRISTMAS season. In some families, the eldest daughter puts on a white dress with a red sash early in the morning. On her head she wears a crown of lingonberry leaves and either four, seven, or nine candles. Other girls in the family also wear white dresses and have halos of tinsel. Boys wear white robes and cone-shaped silver hats, and carry wands with stars on the tips. The "Lucia Bride" wakes the rest of the household by singing a special song. The family then enjoys coffee and buns. A favorite bun is called *lussekatter,* or Lucia cats. The dough is shaped like a cat with raisins for eyes.

Today Swedish immigrants have spread the traditions to Denmark, Finland, Norway, and the United States. Most Swedish groups choose a Lucia Bride who leads the community in the festivities. The Lucias also visit hospitals and nursing homes to cheer the sick and elderly. *See* DIWALI, ST. PATRICK'S DAY, SUMMER SOLSTICE, *and* VALENTINE'S DAY.

Children wear candles and white clothes during St. Lucia's Day, the Festival of Light.

St. Patrick's Day

Saint Patrick's Day is celebrated on March 17 in Ireland and the United States.

Although he is known as the patron saint of Ireland, Saint Patrick was not Irish. He was born to a wealthy family around A.D. 385 in Britannia, the area that is now England. His birth name was Maewyn. When he was a boy, Irish raiders kidnapped him, took him to Ireland, and forced him to work as a shepherd.

Before this time, Maewyn had not been a religious person. Once he was alone, he spent his days as a shepherd, wandering the countryside and praying. He thought he was being punished for having ignored God. One day while he was praying, he heard a voice saying, "Your ship is ready for you." He ran away to the port and found a ship bound for England.

When he returned home, he studied religion. In 432, Pope Celestine I made him a bishop and gave him the name Patercius, or Patrick. Soon after, Patrick had another vision telling him to return to Ireland to start churches and convert the Irish to Christianity. The Irish worshiped many gods and were very close to nature. Patrick used the common three-leaf clover, or shamrock, to illustrate the three parts of the Christian God—Father, Son, and Holy Spirit. By the time of his death in 464, Christianity had spread all over Ireland. Now Saint Patrick is the patron saint of the Irish.

In Ireland Saint Patrick's Day is a holy day and people go to church. In the United States, it is more festive than religious. Most cities hold large parades with bands playing Irish music. It is considered bad luck not to wear something green on this day. Often food and drinks are colored green. The water in the Chicago River is dyed green for the day. Traditional Irish foods are served, such as corned beef and cabbage, Mulligan stew, and Irish soda bread. *See* VALENTINE'S DAY *and* OUR LADY OF FATIMA DAY.

The largest St. Patrick's Day parade in North America is held in New York City. The parade is attended by thousands of people and passes in front of the famous St. Patrick's Cathedral on Fifth Avenue.

Sukkot

Sukkot begins five days after YOM KIPPUR, on the fourteenth day of Tishri (September–October), and lasts for eight days. It is celebrated by Jewish communities around the world. Sukkot is also known as the Feast of Tabernacles and the Feast of Booths.

Sukkot is a Hebrew word meaning "huts" or "small tents." The holiday originated thousands of years ago when Moses and the Jewish people wandered through the desert after their escape from slavery in Egypt. They lived in *sukkot* made of branches, which could easily be taken down and carried as they moved around the desert. After forty years, when the people reached Israel, God told them to hold a special feast each year and live in huts for seven days to remind them of the years in the desert.

In Israel the Jewish people began to farm. Since Sukkot came at the same time of year as the harvest, the holiday became a time to give thanks. Today small huts are built near synagogues and in people's yards. Most Jews no longer live in the huts during the eight days of Sukkot. Instead they may eat all their meals in it or use it as a place to pray. The walls of the huts are made of sweet-smelling branches, and the roof is made of twigs so the stars can be seen through it. The sides are decorated with fruit, vegetables, and blooming flowers. Four kinds of plants are used in Sukkot ceremonies: a palm branch, citron (a type of lemon), myrtle twigs, and willow branches. These plants represent the different ways Jewish people observe or fail to observe the Torah, or law. Tied together, they are called a *lulav,* and they are waved north, south, east, west, up, and down to show that God is everywhere.

Shemini Atzeret falls on the eighth day of Sukkot. It is the day when Jewish people traditionally pray for rain, which is necessary to assure good harvests the next year. It is also a day to hold special services for people who have died. *See* THANKSGIVING.

This man holds a lulav, *or sheaf of symbolic plants, in remembrance of the hardships that the Jewish people endured in the desert.*

The Summer Solstice is celebrated on June 20, 21, or 22 in the northern hemisphere and December 20, 21, or 22 in the southern hemisphere.

The Summer Solstice is significant because it is the longest day of the year. It is light for more hours in the day because the sun is at the farthest point from the equator. After the Summer Solstice, the days grow shorter and the nights longer. The word *solstice* comes from a Latin word meaning "stopping the sun."

The Summer Solstice has been celebrated since ancient times. The earliest evidence comes from ancient Egypt. The Temple of Amen-Ra at Karnak was built in such a way that on the Summer Solstice, a ray of light would shine through a small opening for two to three minutes. The appearance of this light allowed Egyptian scholars to calculate accurately the number of days in the year.

In Europe people lit bonfires on the Summer Solstice to protect themselves from evil spirits that seemed to be taking away the daylight. In Denmark, Norway, and Scotland, people surrounded their cattle with fire to prevent them from catching diseases. In Germany people watched bonfires through branches to keep their eyes healthy. Bonfires were also associated with courtship. In Bohemia young girls looked through wreaths to see the man they would marry and whether their husbands would be faithful. Then they threw the wreaths across the fire to their sweethearts. The singed wreaths were preserved to protect people from illness and bad weather.

Marriage ceremonies were also held on the day of the Summer Solstice. Often these were symbolic marriages, and the couples did not stay married after the festival. The ceremony involved pots of

These modern Druids, followers of an ancient religious order, held a ceremony at Stonehenge in England on the Summer Solstice. The ruins are almost 4,000 years old and are oriented toward the rising sun on the Summer Solstice.

sprouting grain as a symbol of the fertility of nature. Ancient peoples believed that these marriage ceremonies helped combine the forces of nature and society to make the harvests successful

Because the days start getting shorter and the sun disappears for longer and longer periods each night, the time was also popular for symbolic funerals. In Russia people made a straw dummy representing the sun and threw it into a bonfire. Then they held a funeral to mourn the "death" of the sun.

In ancient times, people were much more aware of the cycles of the sun than we are today. They depended on the sun for light and warmth and to help the crops grow. Ceremonies for the Summer Solstice are not practiced much today, athough some groups still hold festivals on the day. *See* VERNAL EQUINOX.

The sundial was used to tell time as far back as 2000 B.C. It consists of a plane (the dial face) and a gnomon (a flat piece of metal that sticks up from the plane).

A Time for Healing

The Summer Solstice was an important time for healers. People believed that herbs collected at this time would be stronger and better for curing diseases. They also believed that some herbs protected them against evil. Herbs collected on this day came to be called St. John's herbs because June 24 is St. John the Baptist's Day.

Mugwort was believed to cure rheumatism and fevers. It was gathered and made into garlands. Its dried leaves were believed to induce wild dreams.

Verbena was typically gathered after sunset and soaked overnight in water. Dried, it was worn around the neck to strengthen the nervous system and relieve stress.

Saint-John's-wort blooms with yellow flowers around the time of the Summer Solstice. The flowers have a strong odor that was believed to drive evil spirits away. It was also used to create oil to treat sunburn.

Hawkweed, or mouse-ear, yields a milky, reddish juice that was used for curing whooping cough and respiratory diseases.

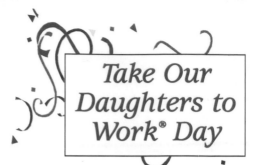

Take Our Daughters to Work® Day

Take Our Daughters to Work® Day is held each year on the fourth Thursday in April in the United States.

The day was created by the Ms. Foundation for Women in 1993. It is an opportunity for girls ages nine to fifteen to go to work with an adult and observe women in a professional environment.

Take Our Daughters to Work® Day was created to show girls all the positive possibilities for the future and to encourage them to focus on their abilities. The Ms. Foundation for Women also hopes to draw national attention to the inequalities women still face in the workplace. Although women make up 46 percent of total paid workers, only 2 percent have top positions at their companies, and many are paid less than their male coworkers.

Each year on this day, millions of girls go to work with adults. Companies participate in many different ways. At the United Nations headquarters, for instance, girls discuss human rights issues and listen to women speakers in the General Assembly Hall. American Airlines allows girls to experience flying a plane by simulator. Actresses give talks at Fox Studios in Los Angeles, and the girls watch the filming of movies. Take Our Daughters to Work® Day has been very successful. As a result, many business and community leaders have created programs to help keep girls on the road to a bright future. *See* CHILDREN'S DAY *and* DOLL FESTIVAL.

Girls get a chance to see the kinds of job opportunities that are available to women on Take Our Daughters to Work® Day. This girl learns what is involved in preparing an operating room for surgery.

Tet Nguyen Dan

See VIETNAMESE NEW YEAR.

Texas Independence Day

Texas Independence Day, also known as Sam Houston Day and Texas Flag Day, is held on March 2 in the state of Texas. It celebrates the events that led to Texas's independence from Mexico. Texas is the only state to celebrate independence from a country other than England.

In the 1820s and 1830s, Texas was a province of Mexico. Immigrants from the United States, as well as some from Mexico, called for independence and began a revolution. The Mexican army, under President Antonio López de Santa Anna, was strong and won many victories. The most notable was at the Alamo, a fort in San Antonio where all the Texan defenders were killed.

The armies continued to fight. Meanwhile, a delegation met at Washington-on-the-Brazos in 1836 to discuss plans for the formal separation of Texas from Mexico. On March 2, they declared independence and unveiled a constitution for the Republic of Texas. On March 4, Sam Houston was appointed commander-in-chief of the Texas military. On April 21, 1836, the Texan troops defeated the Mexican army in the Battle of San Jacinto, captured Santa Anna, and won their independence. Texas existed as an independent country for the next nine years. It became part of the United States in 1846.

Today Texans celebrate both their independence from Mexico and Sam Houston's birthday, which happens to be on the same day. The events leading up to independence are reenacted each year during Texas Week. On March 2, communities have parades and fireworks, and the Texas flag flies all over the state. *See* INDEPENDENCE DAY *and* MEXICAN INDEPENDENCE DAY.

Each year Texans hold parades and fireworks displays to honor the day that Texas declared its independence from Mexico. In 1986 people came from all over the state to Austin, the capital, to celebrate the 150th anniversary of independence.

Thanksgiving

Thanksgiving is celebrated in the United States on the last Thursday in November. In Canada Thanksgiving is on the second Monday in October.

In the 1600s, people called Puritans felt they were persecuted for their religious beliefs in England. They did not believe in the Church of England, which was the official religion of England. Many decided to go to the New World, or America, where they could practice their religion freely.

In 1620 the Pilgrims, as the Puritans who left England were called, began the voyage across the Atlantic Ocean. After sixty-five days at sea, they reached the shores of what is now Massachusetts and made a settlement at Plymouth.

The Pilgrims worked hard the first year in their new country. Because they had never lived in the wilderness before, they did not know how to survive. Many people got sick and died. An Indian named Squanto became friends with the Pilgrims. He had been sold as a slave by English settlers in Virginia but finally escaped to Massachusetts. He showed the Pilgrims how to grow vegetables, such as corn, and the best places for hunting wild game and picking nuts and berries.

With Squanto's help, the Pilgrims had a big harvest and enough food to last the winter. They were so thankful that they held a feast. They invited Squanto and Massasoit, the chief of the local Wampanoag tribe. The Indians brought ninety people and contributed to the feast by offering the meat of five deer. The Pilgrims and Indians feasted for three days. They played games and told stories. It was a great celebration, but there were no plans to make Thanksgiving a yearly event.

The next year, there was not much food, and the Pilgrims did not give thanks. However, the harvest was better the following year, and a celebration was held again. Thanksgiving feasts spread to the other parts of America. Because these celebrations occurred whenever the harvest was complete, some places held Thanksgiving in October and others celebrated it in November.

Pumpkins and gourds are associated with Thanksgiving because they are autumnal crops.

Two hundred years later, well after the founding of the United States, a woman named Sarah Hale wanted the whole country to give thanks at the same time. For many years she wrote letters to politicians and printed Thanksgiving articles in the magazine she edited. Finally, during the Civil War, President Abraham Lincoln proclaimed the last Thursday in November Thanksgiving Day.

Since people no longer have to grow all their food, Thanksgiving is no longer a harvest festival. Instead, it is a time when families in the United States and Canada get together and feast on turkey, stuffing, and other foods. It is a time for everyone to give thanks for all the good things in their lives. One custom associated with the turkey has to do with the wishbone. Once the wishbone is dried, two people make wishes, take hold of the sides, and pull. The bone snaps, and the wish of the person holding the larger half will come true. Some people believe this custom can be traced back to the Romans.

A traditional decoration during Thanksgiving is the cornucopia, a word from Latin meaning "horn of plenty." It is a symbol of abundance and fertility. Many legends are associated with the cornucopia. In Greek mythology, the god Zeus broke off a goat's horn and gave it to his foster mother in appreciation for all she had given him. He told her that the horn would always provide her with anything she needed. In ancient Rome, a goat's horn filled with fruit and other foods was a symbol of Flora, the goddess of flowers, and Fortuna, the goddess of fortune.

In ancient Greece and Rome, harvest festivals often included parades, with wagons decorated with food and wheat. The tradition continued in America. Today the biggest Thanksgiving Day parade is sponsored by Macy's department store in New York City. Giant balloons of popular cartoon characters float down the street. Colorful floats and marching bands participate. *See* SUKKOT.

Many families in the United States and Canada celebrate Thanksgiving by gathering for a feast and giving thanks for all the good things in their lives.

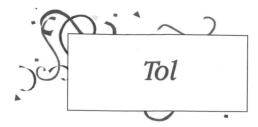

Tol

In Korea, families celebrate two important events in a young child's life. The *paegil* is a holiday celebrated when the child reaches his or her 100th day. The *tol* is the celebration of a baby's first birthday. People view these as special days because, especially in the past, many infants died before reaching those ages.

During the *paegil,* families offer food and drink to Samshin Halmoni, the grandmother spirit. Then they celebrate with rice cakes, fruit, wine, and other treats. The child is dressed in traditional clothes, and games are played. Before they leave, guests are given packages of rice cakes. Parents believe that sharing these treats with others will bring health and happiness to the child.

Tol is important because it is when babies pick their future. The child sits at a table covered with objects, and the item he or she picks is believed to tell what will happen later in his or her life. A baby who picks string will live a long time. One who picks money or rice will have a business career. Choosing cake or other food predicts a career in government service. If a musical instrument is picked, the baby will be an artist.

A special rice cake soup is served at the first birthday party and each year that follows. In Korea if you want to know how old someone is, you ask, "How many rice-cake soups have been eaten in your honor?" *See* CHILDREN'S DAY *and* DOLL FESTIVAL.

Tol is a happy celebration for Korean families, marking the first of many healthy years in a baby's life.

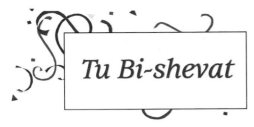

Tu Bi-shevat

Tu Bi-shevat is a Jewish holiday celebrated on the fifteenth day of the month of Shevat, which falls between January 16 and February 13. The day is also known as the Trees' New Year. The holiday originated in Israel, where, because of its climate, Shevat is considered the beginning of spring.

Trees have had special meaning for Jews since ancient times. Different trees symbolize certain characteristics of people. For example, the olive tree represents wisdom, the grapevine symbolizes joy and childbearing, and the palm symbolizes beauty.

Tu Bi-shevat is celebrated by planting trees. In parts of the world where it is too cold for planting, money is collected to buy new trees in Israel. Passages from the Hebrew Scriptures and songs about trees, flowers, and fruit are emphasized. Special foods include fruits that grow in Israel, such as dates, almonds, figs, lemons, and Jaffa oranges. *See* ARBOR DAY *and* MAY DAY.

David Ben-Gurion, Israel's first prime minister, helped celebrate Tu Bi-shevat by watering a newly planted tree.

Vaisakhi

Vaisakhi is a Sikh religious holiday that is celebrated on the first day of the Hindu month Vaisakha, which falls during April. It is most commonly celebrated in India and Malaysia.

The first day of Vaisakhi is the beginning of the New Year and an important date in Sikh history. It commemorates the day that Guru Gobind Singh founded the militant group Khalsa in 1699. Singh's teachings are the basis of much of the Sikh religion. Vaisakhi continues to be the principal time for initiating new members into Khalsa. The day also commemorates the decision in 1747 to build a permanent fortress at Amritsar. The city has become a major center of the Sikh religion.

To celebrate Vaisakhi, Sikhs must visit the largest place of worship they can. Many flock to the Golden Temple in Amritsar. Continuous reading of the Granth Sahib, the Sikh holy book, goes on for forty-eight hours. After religious ceremonies, there is feasting and folk dancing. In the Golden Temple, people bathe in the Pool of Immortality. In northern India, Vaisakhi is also a harvest festival. People participate in a dance called the *bhangra,* which reenacts the entire harvest. *See* IRANIAN NEW YEAR *and* ROSH HASHANAH.

Valentine's Day

People have celebrated Valentine's Day on February 14 for centuries. It is especially popular in England, France, Canada, and the United States.

The origins of this holiday celebrating love and friendship go back to two Roman holidays. One, Lupercalia, honored the god Lupercus, who guarded Rome from wolves. The other honored Juno, queen of the Roman gods. On this day, young men picked the names of girls from a bowl, and the matched couples celebrated the holiday together. As Christianity spread, these two holidays became mixed with a Christian holiday honoring Saint Valentine.

There are many legends about Saint Valentine. In one story, Valentine was jailed for helping Christians who were being persecuted. While in jail, he cured a guard's daughter of blindness. Despite this miracle, he was sentenced to death. The night before he was killed, he wrote a loving note to the young girl and signed it, "From your Valentine." Saint Valentine died on February 14, and his name was given to the holiday.

Often valentine notes are decorated with hearts. Long ago, people thought their feelings came from their hearts, so the heart became a symbol of feelings of love. Another symbol is Cupid, the Roman god of love. He is usually shown as a chubby little boy who shoots arrows into people's hearts, making them fall in love with the next person they see.

Valentine's Day first became popular in the United States in the 1860s, during the Civil War. Soldiers sent thousands of valentines to their sweethearts from faraway camps and battlefields.

Many superstitions surround the day. Some people think that the first person you see on this day will be your valentine. It is good luck to be awakened by a kiss. It is also thought that if you dream of someone the night before Valentine's Day, that person will be your sweetheart. *See* ST. PATRICK'S DAY.

In the 1700s, young men and women drew names from a valentine box and wore the names pinned to their sleeves for all of Valentine's Day. Today we use the valentine box to give cards to and receive cards from friends or classmates.

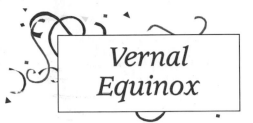

Vernal Equinox

El Castillo (the Pyramid of Kukulcan) in the Yucatan, is a popular place where people gather for the Vernal Equinox.

The Vernal Equinox is observed on March 20, 21, or 22 in the northern hemisphere and on September 20, 21, or 22 in the southern hemisphere. Its name comes from Latin words meaning "of spring" and "equal day and night." Around the globe, on the March and September dates, the day is the same length as the night. This is because the sun is crossing the equator. March marks spring in the northern hemisphere and autumn in the southern hemisphere. September marks the Autumnal Equinox in the northern hemisphere and spring in the southern hemisphere.

The Vernal Equinox signals the beginning of spring when the days start getting longer and warmer weather begins. In ancient times, the equinox was considered the beginning of the year, and people celebrated by fasting and feasting, ringing bells, and cleaning house. *See* SUMMER SOLSTICE.

Vesak

Vesak is held on the first full moon of the Hindu month Vaisakha (during April or May). It is celebrated by Buddhists around the world.

Vesak honors the Buddha, Siddhartha Gautama. He was born in 563 B.C. to a wealthy family, but he was not happy. He gave up his wealth and wandered around the world seeking fulfillment. One morning, while meditating, he achieved enlightenment, or Nirvana, meaning that he saw the world from a different perspective and found deeper meaning in his life. From that vision, he designed a new religious system that allowed people to free themselves from the concerns of the world and to reach Nirvana. He had many followers and became known as the Buddha, or enlightened one.

On Vesak, Buddhists bathe statues of the Buddha. The custom originates from a legend that two serpents bathed him at his birth. In China his statue is placed in a jug of water, and people sprinkle a spoonful of water over his head. In Japan they bathe the Buddha's image in *ama-cha*, a sweet tea. In all Buddhist communities, believers gather in temples and decorate their homes with paper lanterns and lamps. Because Buddhists believe in being kind to all living creatures, it is traditional to free caged birds. People also make pilgrimages to the place of the Buddha's birth, Lumbini, Nepal. *See* MUHAMMAD'S BIRTHDAY *and* CONFUCIUS'S BIRTHDAY.

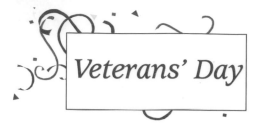

Veterans' Day

Veterans' Day is celebrated on November 11 in the United States, Canada, England, and France.

On November 11, 1918, an armistice, or truce, was signed ending World War I. Eight years later, in 1926, a holiday was started in honor of the soliders who fought in the war. It was called Armistice Day. As part of the ceremonies, the remains of an unknown American soldier were buried at Arlington National Cemetery. Similar events took place in England and France, at each nation's highest place of honor (Westminster Abbey in England and the Arc de Triomphe in France).

When World War I ended, it was called the war to end all wars. Unfortunately, World War II and other wars followed. It was decided that Armistice Day should honor soldiers from all these conflicts. In 1954, President Dwight D. Eisenhower proclaimed November 11 as Veterans' Day. (A veteran is a former soldier.) In 1958, two more unknown soldiers, one from World War II and one from the Korean War, were placed in the Tomb of the Unknowns at Arlington National Cemetery.

Today the Tomb of the Unknowns is still the site of the national ceremonies for Veterans' Day. All year long, guards keep watch over the monument, and a flame burns day and night, as it has since 1926.

Veterans' Day observances also take place all over the country, especially in places that had significance during a war, such as battleships and naval stations. Typical celebrations include parades, speeches, military balls, and religious services. Poppies are also used as a symbol of Veterans' Day. The red flowers grew on many battlegrounds in Europe during World War I and came to symbolize the bloodshed that took place there. Veterans' organizations sell poppies on this day and use the money to care for veterans. The flower is also used to decorate the graves of soldiers. *See* ANZAC DAY *and* MEMORIAL DAY.

The Tomb of the Unknowns is the site of an annual Veterans' Day salute. The tomb contains the bodies of unknown soldiers from America's wars, each representing the sacrifices of countless other soldiers.

Victoria Day

Victoria Day is celebrated on the Monday that preceeds or falls on May 24 in Canada. It honors Queen Victoria of England and is held on her birthday.

Victoria ascended the English throne in 1838, when she was eighteen years old. Despite having led an isolated childhood, Victoria took the throne with great grace and dignity.

In February 1840, Queen Victoria married Prince Albert of Saxe-Coburg Gotha, her first cousin. Over the next ten years, they had eight children. Victoria was a devoted mother. She became a symbol of virtue and dignity, but also of formality.

Victoria ruled during a time of great advances for England. The Industrial Revolution had brought about many new machines and technologies. Queen Victoria realized the importance of technology. She encouraged Albert to organize the Great Exhibition of 1851, a showcase of technology that was visited by more than six million people during its six-month run.

After Albert died in 1861, Victoria found it difficult to fulfill her duties as queen. However, she realized how much a strong leader was needed. She enjoyed foreign affairs and was proud of England's growing influence around the world. Once again she proved to be a great leader.

Queen Victoria died on January 22, 1901, at the age of eighty-one. She had ruled England longer than anyone in British history. Her children and their descendants ruled many places in Europe, including Germany, Russia, and Spain. Because of this, Victoria received the nickname "grandmother of Europe." For her honesty, patriotism, and devotion, Victoria became the symbol of the solidarity of the British Empire. Her reign is often called the Victorian Era.

It was during Victoria's reign that Canada was organized as an independent country. Her birthday is celebrated there with many different events. In Victoria, B.C., maypole dancing and a May Queen are part of the celebration. In southern Canada, it is a day for Canadians to plant the garden. Since 1900 Newfoundland has celebrated this holiday with trout fishing. *See* KING KAMEHAMEHA I DAY.

This statue, which honors Queen Victoria, stands in Canada.

Vietnamese New Year (Tet Nguyen Dan)

Vietnamese New Year, or Tet, begins on the first day of the lunar New Year and lasts for seven days. It usually falls in late January or early February. The official name is Tet Nguyen Dan, which means "first day" in Vietnamese.

The festivities begin on the last night of the old year, when the Kitchen God is said to report to the Jade Emperor how the family has behaved all year. To help the Kitchen God on his journey and to protect themselves from evil spirits during his absence, families set up a Cay Neu. The Cay Neu is a bamboo pole stripped of all leaves except for a few on top. It is displayed in front of the house during the holiday. At midnight the Kitchen God returns and is welcomed with fireworks, gongs, and drums. It is now the beginning of the New Year.

On the first day of the New Year, altars are arranged to honor the family's ancestors. Special food and drink are prepared for the spirits, who return to spend a few days with the family. Families and friends spend the second day visiting each other. On the third day, people honor their past teachers. On the fourth day, the ancestors leave. Families visit graveyards and perform ceremonies to help their ancestors get back to the land of the dead. During the final three days, people go back to work and life returns to normal, although it is still a time of celebration.

It is believed that the events of the first day of the New Year set the tone for the year. People pay off old debts, buy new clothes, and paint their houses. The first person to visit a household is thought to influence its fortune for the year. Families invite wealthy or powerful people to stop by early in the day and encourage those who might be unlucky to wait until later. Everyone tries to be cheerful and optimistic. *See* CHINESE NEW YEAR, IRANIAN NEW YEAR, *and* NEW YEAR'S DAY.

Women pray at a shrine during Tet to help their ancestors get back to the land of the dead.

Waitangi Day

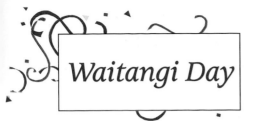

On Waitangi Day and other holidays, Maori people hold large gatherings called hui. *One traditional dance is called an action song.*

Waitangi Day is observed on February 6 in New Zealand. In 1769 Captain James Cook became the first European to explore New Zealand. By 1830 the number of settlers had grown, and leaders in England realized they needed a government. They sent William Hobson to claim the islands as part of the Australian colony of New South Wales.

However, the native people of New Zealand, the Maori, did not want to give up their land. The two groups fought as the English took the Maori land. On February 6, 1840, the British forced the Maori to sign a treaty recognizing Queen Victoria as their ruler. The Maori were given full rights as English citizens. The treaty is now known as the Treaty of Waitangi because it was signed in the town of Waitangi on the Bay of Islands.

Each year people wear nineteenth-century costumes and reenact the signing of the treaty. Traditional Maori stories are told and acted out. Maori arts are taught, such as dancing, singing, and weaving. Because the treaty ended Maori control of their land, some people believe it is wrong to celebrate. The holiday has become less popular in recent years. However, most people focus on the peaceful coexistence of the Maori and the people of English descent. *See* ATI-ATIHAN FESTIVAL.

Walpurgisnacht (Walpurgis Night)

Walpurgisnacht is celebrated on the night of April 30 in Germany, Austria, and the Scandinavian countries.

On this night, it is believed that witches meet on Brocken, the tallest peak of the Harz Mountains in Germany. To protect themselves and frighten away the witches, people ring church bells and carry burning torches. They also wear witch costumes and hold parties. In Sweden people build huge bonfires on hilltops. They believe that the fields and crops will be blessed for as far as the glow of the fire reaches.

The day is named for St. Walpurga, an eighth-century nun. On this day, her remains were moved from Heidenheim, Germany, to Eichstatt, Germany (Bavaria), which has become a popular place for pilgrimages. It is believed that her name has become confused with that of Waldborg, an ancient fertility goddess. *See* HALLOWEEN.

World AIDS Day

World AIDS Day is observed on December 1 around the world. The holiday was created in 1988 by the World Health Organization of the United Nations to promote awareness of AIDS and its prevention, control, research, and education.

AIDS stands for acquired immuno-deficiency syndrome. It is a fairly new disease that scientists believe originated in central Africa. The first cases were discovered in the United States in the early 1980s. Since then, 27.9 million people around the world have been infected by the virus and 5.8 million, including 1.3 million children, have died.

AIDS is believed to be caused by a virus called the human immunodeficiency virus (HIV). A virus lives inside healthy cells in the body and destroys them. After HIV enters the system, it attaches itself to white blood cells, which are part of the immune system. As the virus reproduces, the immune system is weakened. This means the body cannot fight diseases. Although there is no cure yet, many new drugs are being tested to treat HIV. Scientists are also trying to discover a vaccine to keep people from becoming infected with the virus.

The efforts of many people have helped spread awareness about AIDS. One example is the NAMES Project, a huge quilt made in memory of those who have died from AIDS. By 1989, the AIDS quilt had more than 11,000 panels and weighed thirteen tons. It has raised millions of dollars for the care of people with AIDS.

To slow the spread of the disease, people need to learn how to protect themselves. A person cannot catch AIDS from casual contact, such as hugging or shaking hands. It is spread through the exchange of body fluids, usually during sexual intercourse or when sharing needles for drug use. Many organizations have been created to educate people about the disease.

On World AIDS Day, many schools hold workshops on AIDS. Medical professionals discuss stereotypes and myths people often believe about the disease. People with AIDS talk about their experiences living with the disease.

The day is also important for raising money to help those who are suffering from the disease live a better life and to fund the research that will one day lead to a cure. *See* EARTH DAY *and* PAN-AMERICAN DAY.

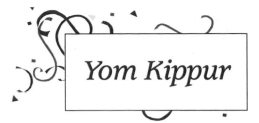

Yom Kippur

Yom Kippur is celebrated seven days after ROSH HASHANAH. It ends on the tenth day of the month Tishri (September–October). It is considered the most important day of the Jewish year and has been celebrated for thousands of years.

The name *Yom Kippur* means "Day of Atonement." To atone means to make up for a wrong one has done. On this day, Jewish people ask God to forgive them their sins of the past year.

Before Yom Kippur begins, people eat a large meal and prepare for a long fast. When the meal is finished and the sun has set, a candle is lit to signify that the holiday has begun. That night Jews go to the temple to pray. A special prayer, which is sung, called the *Kol Nidre* opens the service. The words *Kol Nidre* mean "all vows." The prayer asks God to forgive the false promises people make when they are not thinking clearly.

The shofar, *made from a curved ram's horn, has been used for more than 6,000 years and is an important part of both* ROSH HASHANAH *and Yom Kippur.*

The next day, services are held in the synagogue. Jews take the day off from work or school and pray. Often special prayers are said for children. All day people refrain from eating or drinking. At the end of the day, the *shofar* is blown to signal the end of the holiday. *See* LENT.

Calendars from Around the World

Since the beginning of civilization, people around the world have measured time by years, months, and days. Evidence of the earliest calendars can be seen at Stonehenge in England and the pyramids in Egypt, where people erected structures aligned with the rising sun. As soon as people were able to track time, they could predict the changes in seasons and know when to plant and harvest crops. Early civilizations based their calendars upon the cycles of the moon and sun. The calendars used today measure time in the same way, but because modern calculations are much more exact, calendars are more accurate.

The Roman Calendar

The original Roman calendar was developed in the seventh century B.C. It divided the year into ten months, with a total of 304 days. Two more months, January and February, were added later. However, the number of days in the year still did not add up to the amount of time it takes Earth to travel around the sun. To make up the difference, an extra month was added every other year. The addition of days or months to a calendar is called intercalation.

The Julian Calendar

In 46 B.C., Julius Caesar decided to reform the Roman calendar system. At that time, the old Roman calendar was about three months ahead of the seasons. Holidays that traditionally occurred in spring were now falling in summer. The calendar said it was winter when the weather said it was autumn. Farmers could not rely on the calendar to determine planting and harvesting times. To make the correct adjustments, the year 46 B.C. was given 445 days. It was known as *ultimus annus confusionis,* which means "the last year of confusion."

The new calendar had 365 days, with an additional day every four years in February. This was very close to the actual time it takes Earth to move around the sun (365.242199 days). The Julian calendar was used for more than 1,600 years. However, there was still a slight discrepancy in the solar cycle, and by 1582 there was a ten-day difference between the season and the date. Once again holidays were occurring in the wrong seasons.

The Gregorian Calendar

Pope Gregory XIII ordered a reform of the Julian calendar in the sixteenth century. To adjust it, he deleted ten days from the year 1582, making the calendar skip from October 5 to October 15. He also determined that there were too many leap year days—the extra day every fourth February. Under the Gregorian calendar, there is no leap year day in years ending in 00 unless the year is divisible by 400.

With these changes, the Gregorian calendar became a very accurate measure of time and seasons. When it was first developed, it was used only in Roman Catholic countries. Today it is used around the world. Many cultures, however, use different calendars to track religious holidays.

The Jewish Calendar

The present Jewish calendar was developed more than 2,300 years ago by Hillel I. It has twelve months that alternate between twenty-nine and thirty days in length. The Jewish calendar is based on the lunar cycle, the appearance of the new moon. Because this is shorter than the solar cycle (the path of Earth around the sun), the days are not consistent with the seasons. A thirteenth month is added seven times within a cycle of nineteen years in order to adjust the calendar. Lunar calendars that make adjustments to keep up with the solar cycle are known as lunisolar calendars.

Year 1 of the Jewish calendar marks the date of creation. It is believed to correspond with 3761 B.C. in the Gregorian calendar, so the year 2000 is 5761 in the Jewish calendar. The years are followed by the abbreviation A.M., which stands for *anno mundi* (year of the world).

The Jewish months (and the corresponding Gregorian calendar months) are:

☆ Tishri (September–October)
☆ Heshvan (October–November)
☆ Kislev (November–December)
☆ Tebeth (December–January)
☆ Shevat (January–February)
☆ Adar (February–March)
☆ Nisan (March–April)
☆ Iyar (April–May)
☆ Sivan (May–June)
☆ Tammuz (June–July)
☆ Ab (July–August)
☆ Ellul (August–September)

The Hindu Calendar

The Hindu calendar consists of 360 days divided into twelve months of thirty days each. Every five years, a leap month is added in order to keep the calendar in line with the seasons. The months are counted from full moon to full moon. Each month is divided into two parts: Krsna (when the moon is waning, or getting smaller) and Sukla (when the moon is waxing, or getting fuller). Different Hindu groups recognize different eras, making the year 2000 anywhere from 5102 to 1922 in the Hindu calendar.

The Hindu months (and the corresponding Gregorian calendar months) are:

- ☆ Chaitra (March–April)
- ☆ Vaisakha (April–May)
- ☆ Jyaistha (May–June)
- ☆ Asadha (June–July)
- ☆ Sravana (July–August)
- ☆ Bhadrapada (August–September)
- ☆ Asvina (September–October)
- ☆ Kartika (October–November)
- ☆ Margasirsa (November–December)
- ☆ Pausa (December–January)
- ☆ Magha (January–February)
- ☆ Phalguna (February–March)

The Chinese Calendar

The Chinese calendar begins at the equivalent of 2637 B.C., when the Emperor Huangdi is said to have invented it. That is the Chinese year 1. This calendar is counted in cycles of sixty. The years within each cycle are broken down into five repeating twelve-year cycles. In these cycles, each year is named after one of ten Chinese constellations and one of twelve animals. The animals are the rat, ox, tiger, hare, dragon, snake, horse, sheep, monkey, rooster, dog, and pig. The year 2000 (or 4637 in the Chinese calendar) is the year of the dragon.

The Chinese year is based on the cycles of the moon. Each year consists of about twelve months. Each month begins with the new moon and has twenty-nine or thirty days. A month is repeated seven times during each nineteen-year period. This keeps the calendar in line with the seasons. The year starts at the second new moon after the beginning of winter in the northern hemisphere. Chinese New Year never occurs earlier than January 20 or later than February 20.

The Islamic Calendar

The Islamic calendar is based solely on the phases of the moon. No adjustments are made to keep up with the solar cycle. Because of this, the dates of holidays move backward about ten days each year when compared to the season. For example, if Ramadan occurs in winter one year, eighteen years later it will occur in summer. Many Islamic countries use the Gregorian calendar for political and civil purposes and the Islamic calendar to determine the dates of religious holidays.

The Islamic calendar begins with year 1, which corresponds to July 16, 622. On this date, the prophet Muhammad went into an exile known as *hejira*. The years are followed by the abbreviation A.H., which stands for *anno Hegirae* (year of the *hejira*). The year 2000 is the year 1378 A.H. in the Islamic calendar.

The Islamic months are:

☆ Muharram
☆ Safar
☆ Rabi' al-awwal (Rabi' I)
☆ Rabi' al-thani (Rabi' II)
☆ Jumada al-awwal (Jumada I)
☆ Jumada al-thani (Jumada II)
☆ Rajab
☆ Sha'ban
☆ Ramadan
☆ Shawwal
☆ Dhu al-Qi'dah
☆ Dhu al-Hijja

Holiday Calendar

	2001	2002	2003	2004	2005
Jan.	1 New Year's Day/ Emancipation Day/ Korean New Year 2 Berchtold's Day 6 Epiphany 11 Hostos Day 15 Adults' Day/ Martin Luther King Jr. Day/ Robert E. Lee Day 20 Ati-Atihan Festival begins 24 Chinese New Year 26 Australia Day	1 New Year's Day/ Emancipation Day/ Korean New Year 2 Berchtold's Day 6 Epiphany 11 Hostos Day 15 Adults' Day 19 Ati-Atihan Festival begins 21 Martin Luther King Jr. Day/ Robert E. Lee Day 26 Australia Day 28 Tu Bi-shevat 29 Full Moon Day/ Korean New Year	1 New Year's Day/ Emancipation Day/ Korean New Year 2 Berchtold's Day 6 Epiphany 11 Hostos Day 15 Adults' Day 18 Ati-Atihan Festival begins/ Tu Bi-shevat 20 Martin Luther King Jr. Day/ Robert E. Lee Day 26 Australia Day	1 New Year's Day/ Emancipation Day/ Korean New Year 2 Berchtold's Day 6 Epiphany 11 Hostos Day 15 Adults' Day 17 Ati-Atihan Festival begins 19 Martin Luther King Jr. Day/ Robert E. Lee Day 22 Chinese New Year 26 Australia Day	1 New Year's Day/ Emancipation Day/ Korean New Year 2 Berchtold's Day 6 Epiphany 11 Hostos Day 15 Adults' Day/ Ati-Atihan Festival begins 17 Martin Luther King Jr. Day/ Robert E. Lee Day 21 Eid al-Adha 25 Tu Bi-shevat/ Full Moon Day/ Korean New Year 26 Australia Day
Feb.	6 Waitangi Day 8 Tu Bi-shevat/ Full Moon Day/ Korean New Year 14 Valentine's Day 19 Presidents' Day 27 Mardi Gras 28 Ash Wednesday/ Lent	6 Waitangi Day 12 Chinese New Year/ Mardi Gras 13 Ash Wednesday/ Lent 14 Valentine's Day 18 Presidents' Day 23 Eid al-Adha 26 Purim	1 Chinese New Year 6 Waitangi Day 12 Eid al-Adha 14 Valentine's Day 17 Presidents' Day/ Full Moon Day/ Korean New Year	2 Eid al-Adha 6 Waitangi Day/ Full Moon Day/ Korean New Year 7 Tu Bi-shevat 14 Valentine's Day 16 Presidents' Day 24 Mardi Gras 25 Ash Wedneday/ Lent 29 Leap Year Day	6 Waitangi Day 8 Mardi Gras 9 Chinese New Year/ Ash Wednesday/ Lent 14 Valentine's Day 19 Ashura 21 Presidents' Day
March	2 Texas Independence Day 3 Doll Festival 6 Eid al-Adha 9 Purim 17 St. Patrick's Day 19 St. Joseph's Day 20 Vernal Equinox/ Iranian New Year	2 Texas Independence Day 3 Doll Festival 17 St. Patrick's Day 19 St. Joseph's Day 20 Vernal Equinox/ Iranian New Year 24 Palm Sunday/ Ashura 28 Passover 29 Good Friday 31 Easter	2 Texas Independence Day 3 Doll Festival 4 Mardi Gras 5 Ash Wednesday/ Lent 14 Ashura 17 St. Patrick's Day 18 Purim 19 St. Joseph's Day 20 Vernal Equinox/ Iranian New Year	2 Texas Independence Day/ Ashura 3 Doll Festival 7 Purim 17 St. Patrick's Day 19 St. Joseph's Day 20 Vernal Equinox/ Iranian New Year	2 Texas Independence Day 3 Doll Festival 17 St. Patrick's Day 19 St. Joseph's Day 20 Palm Sunday 20 Vernal Equinox/ Iranian New Year 25 Good Friday/ Purim 27 Easter

	2001	2002	2003	2004	2005
April	1 April Fools' Day 4 Ashura 8 Palm Sunday/ Passover 13 Vaisakhi/ Good Friday 14 Pan-American Day 15 Easter 16 Sechseläuten begins 20 Holocaust Remembrance Day 22 Earth Day 25 ANZAC Day 26 Take Our Daughters to Work® Day 27 Arbor Day 30 Walpurgisnacht	1 April Fools' Day 9 Holocaust Remembrance Day 13 Vaisakhi 14 Pan-American Day 15 Sechseläuten begins 22 Earth Day 25 ANZAC Day/ Take Our Daughters to Work® Day 26 Arbor Day 27 Vesak 30 Walpurgisnacht	1 April Fools' Day 13 Vaisakhi/ Palm Sunday 14 Pan-America Day 17 Passover/ Vesak 18 Good Friday 20 Easter/ 21 Sechseläuten begins 22 Earth Day 24 Take Our Daughters to Work® Day 25 ANZAC Day/ Arbor Day 29 Holocaust Remembrance Day 30 Walpurgisnacht	1 April Fools' Day 4 Palm Sunday 6 Passover 9 Good Friday 11 Easter 13 Vaisakhi 14 Pan-American Day 18 Holocaust Remembrance Day 19 Sechseläuten begins 22 Earth Day/ Take Our Daughters to Work® Day 25 ANZAC Day 30 Walpurgisnacht/ Arbor Day	1 April Fools' Day 13 Vaisakhi 14 Pan-American Day 18 Sechseläuten begins 21 Muhammad's Birthday 22 Earth Day 24 Passover/ Vesak 25 ANZAC Day 28 Take Our Daughters to Work® Day 29 Arbor Day 30 Walpurgisnacht
May	1 May Day 3 Polish Constitution Day 5 Children's Day/ Cinco de Mayo 7 Vesak 13 Mother's Day 21 Victoria Day 28 Memorial Day 30 Feast of Joan of Arc	1 May Day 3 Polish Constitution Day 5 Children's Day/ Cinco de Mayo 12 Mother's Day 19 Pentecost 20 Victoria Day 25 Muhammad's Birthday 27 Memorial Day 30 Feast of Corpus Christi/ Feast of Joan of Arc	1 May Day 3 Polish Constitution Day 5 Children's Day/ Cinco de Mayo 11 Mother's Day 14 Muhammad's Birthday 19 Victoria Day 26 Memorial Day 30 Feast of Joan of Arc	1 May Day 2 Muhammad's Birthday 3 Polish Constitution Day 5 Children's Day/ Cinco de Mayo/ Vesak 9 Mother's Day 24 Victoria Day 30 Pentecost/Feast of Joan of Arc 31 Memorial Day	1 May Day 3 Polish Constitution Day 5 Children's Day/ Cinco de Mayo 6 Holocaust Remembrance Day 8 Mother's Day 15 Pentecost 23 Victoria Day 26 Feast of Corpus Christi 30 Memorial Day/ Feast of Joan of Arc
June	3 Pentecost 4 Muhammad's Birthday 11 King Kamehameha I Day 12 Philippine Independence Day 14 Flag Day/ Feast of Corpus Christi 17 Father's Day 21 Summer Solstice 24 St. John the Baptist Day 25 Dragon Boat Festival	11 King Kamehameha I Day 12 Philippine Independence Day 14 Flag Day 15 Dragon Boat Festival 16 Father's Day 21 Summer Solstice 24 St. John the Baptist Day	4 Dragon Boat Fetival 8 Pentecost 11 King Kamehameha I Day 12 Philippine Independence Day 14 Flag Day 15 Father's Day 19 Feast of Corpus Christi 21 Summer Solstice 24 St. John the Baptist Day	10 Feast of Corpus Christi 11 King Kamehameha I Day 12 Philippine Independence Day 14 Flag Day 20 Father's Day/ Summer Solstice 22 Dragon Boat Festival 24 St. John the Baptist Day	11 King Kamehameha I Day/ Dragon Boat Festival 12 Philippine Independence Day 14 Flag Day 19 Father's Day 21 Summer Solstice 24 St. John the Baptist Day

	2001	2002	2003	2004	2005
July	1 Canada Day 4 Independence Day 12 Orange Day 13 Our Lady of Fatima Day/ Obon begins 14 Bastille Day 24 Mormon Pioneer Day/ Raksha Bandhama	1 Canada Day 4 Independence Day 12 Orange Day 13 Our Lady of Fatima Day/ Obon begins 14 Bastille Day 24 Mormon Pioneer Day/ Raksha Bandhama	1 Canada Day 4 Independence Day 12 Orange Day 13 Our Lady of Fatima Day/ Obon begins 14 Bastille Day 24 Mormon Pioneer Day/ Raksha Bandhama	1 Canada Day 4 Independence Day 12 Orange Day 13 Our Lady of Fatima Day/ Obon begins 14 Bastille Day 24 Mormon Pioneer Day/ Raksha Bandhama	1 Canada Day 4 Independence Day 12 Orange Day 13 Our Lady of Fatima Day/ Obon begins 14 Bastille Day 24 Mormon Pioneer Day/ Raksha Bandhama
Aug.	13 Central African Republic Independence Day 15 Assumption Day	13 Central African Republic Independence Day 15 Assumption Day	13 Central African Republic Independence Day 15 Assumption Day	13 Central African Republic Independence Day 15 Assumption Day	13 Central African Republic Independence Day 15 Assumption Day
Sept.	3 Labor Day 16 Mexican Independence Day 17 Citizenship Day 18 Rosh Hashana 19 Feast of San Gennaro 22 Autumnal Equinox 27 Yom Kippur 28 Confucius's Birthday/ Dussehra	2 Labor Day 7 Rosh Hashana 16 Mexican Independence Day/ Yom Kippur 17 Citizenship Day 19 Feast of San Gennaro 23 Autumnal Equinox 21 Sukkot 28 Confucius's Birthday/ Dussehra	1 Labor Day 16 Mexican Independence Day 17 Citizenship Day 19 Feast of San Gennaro 23 Autumnal Equinox 27 Rosh Hashana 28 Confucius's Birthday/ Dussehra	6 Labor Day 16 Mexican Independence Day/ Rosh Hashana 17 Citizenship Day 19 Feast of San Gennaro 22 Autumnal Equinox 25 Yom Kippur 28 Confucius's Birthday/ Dussehra 30 Sukkot	5 Labor Day 16 Mexican Independence Day 17 Citizenship Day 19 Feast of San Gennaro 22 Autumnal Equinox 28 Confucius's Birthday/ Dussehra
Oct.	2 Sukkot 8 Columbus Day 11 Pulaski Day 29 Republic Day 31 Halloween/ Diwali	11 Pulaski Day 14 Columbus Day 29 Republic Day 31 Halloween/ Diwali	6 Yom Kippur 11 Pulaski Day/ Sukkot 13 Columbus Day 27 Ramadan begins 29 Republic Day 31 Halloween/Diwali	11 Pulaski Day/ Columbus Day 15 Ramadan begins 29 Republic Day 31 Halloween/ Diwali	4 Rosh Hashana/ Ramadan begins 10 Columbus Day 11 Pulaski Day 13 Yom Kippur 18 Sukkot 29 Republic Day 31 Halloween/Diwali
Nov.	1 All Saints' Day/ Day of the Dead begins 2 All Souls' Day 3 Sadie Hawkins Day 5 Guy Fawkes Day 11 Veterans' Day 17 Ramadan begins 22 Thanksgiving	1 All Saints' Day/ Day of the Dead begins 2 All Souls' Day/ Sadie Hawkins Day 5 Guy Fawkes Day 6 Ramadan begins 11 Veterans' Day 28 Thanksgiving 30 Hanukkah begins	1 All Saints' Day/ Day of the Dead begins/ Sadie Hawkins Day 2 All Souls' Day 5 Guy Fawkes Day 11 Veterans' Day 26 Eid al-Fitr 27 Thanksgiving 30 Advent	1 All Saints' Day/ Day of the Dead begins 2 All Souls' Day 5 Guy Fawkes Day 6 Sadie Hawkins Day 11 Veterans' Day 14 Eid al-Fitr 25 Thanksgiving 28 Advent	1 All Saints' Day/ Day of the Dead begins 2 All Souls' Day 3 Eid al-Fitr 5 Guy Fawkes Day/ Sadie Hawkins Day 11 Veterans' Day 24 Thanksgiving 27 Advent

	2001	**2002**	**2003**	**2004**	**2005**
Dec.	1 World AIDS Day 2 Advent 7 Pearl Harbor Day 10 Hanukkah begins 12 Jamhuri Day 13 St. Lucia's Day 16 Los Posadas begins 17 Eid al-Fitr 21 Winter Solstice 25 Christmas 26 Boxing Day/ Kwanzaa begins	1 World AIDS Day/ Advent 6 Eid al-Fitr 7 Pearl Harbor Day 12 Jamhuri Day 13 St. Lucia's Day 16 Los Posadas begins 21 Winter Solstice 25 Christmas 26 Boxing Day/ Kwanzaa begins	1 World AIDS Day 7 Pearl Harbor Day 12 Jamhuri Day 13 St. Lucia's Day 16 Los Posadas begins 20 Hanukkah begins 22 Winter Solstice 25 Christmas 26 Boxing Day/ Kwanzaa begins	1 World AIDS Day 7 Pearl Harbor Day 8 Hanukkah begins 12 Jamhuri Day 13 St. Lucia's Day 16 Los Posadas begins 21 Winter Solstice 25 Christmas 26 Boxing Day/ Kwanzaa begins	1 World AIDS Day 7 Pearl Harbor Day 12 Jamhuri Day 13 St. Lucia's Day 16 Los Posadas begins 21 Winter Solstice 25 Christmas 26 Boxing Day/ Kwanzaa begins/ Hanukkah begins

Glossary

acronym A word formed from the first letters or groups of letters of a phrase.

altar A raised surface on which offerings to a god or an ancestor can be placed.

ancestors People from whom one is descended.

Assumption The rising of the body of Mary, the mother of Jesus, to heaven.

avatar The form a god or goddess takes on Earth.

ceremony A specific act or ritual that occurs on a certain occasion, such as a holiday, according to traditional rules.

citizen An individual member of a state or country.

commemorate To recall or honor the memory of a person or an event.

custom A long-established or accepted way of doing things.

effigy A representation of a person often used for hanging or burning.

fast The act of not eating or drinking for a certain period of time.

feast days Special days set aside to celebrate a religious anniversary, as by the Christian church to honor the major saints.

heresy An opinion that goes against official beliefs. A heretic is a person who holds these beliefs, usually someone from inside a religious group who goes against the teaching of that group.

honor To show respect to a person or an event.

immersion The act of plunging into water.

incense A substance that is burned to produce a special aroma. It is often used in religious ceremonies.

legend A story from the past told for many years, usually without a known origin.

Mass The main service of worship in the Roman Catholic Church and some other Christian denominations.

pagan A person who follows a religion other than the world's major religions. This once meant someone who worshiped the gods of Greece and Rome.

pilgrimage A journey to a sacred place.

procession People in a group marching or riding forward, as in a parade.

prosperity Good fortune, wealth, and success.

purgatory In Catholicism, the place where souls go after death to make up for their sins before entering heaven.

realm A kingdom.

repentance The act of feeling sorry for a sin or regretting an action.

sacrament Christian rites, such as confession, Holy Communion, and baptism.

sacrifice To give up something of value, either for another person or to show faith or devotion to God.

solstice The points at which the sun is farthest from the earth's equator.

symbol Something that stands for something else. For example, in China peaches represent long life.

Bibliography

Aaseng, Nathan. *Robert E. Lee*. Minneapolis: Lerner Publications Co., 1991.

Behrens, June. *Fiesta! Cinco de Mayo*. Chicago: Children's Press, 1978.

Bernhard, Emery. *Happy New Year!* New York: Lodestar Books, 1996.

Carter, Alden. *The Civil War*. New York: Franklin Watts, 1992.

Coil, Suzanne M. *Mardi Gras!* New York: Macmillan International, 1994.

Drucker, Malka. *Passover: A Season of Freedom*. New York: Holiday House, 1981.

——. *Rosh Hashanah and Yom Kippur: Sweet Beginnings*. New York: Holiday House, 1981.

——. *Sukkot: A Time to Rejoice*. New York: Holiday House, 1982.

Fishman, Cathy. *On Passover*. New York: Atheneum Books for Young Readers, 1997.

Fradin, Dennis B. *Christmas*. Springfield, NJ: Enslow Publishers, 1990.

——. *Thanksgiving Day*. Springfield, NJ: Enslow Publishers, 1990.

——. *Valentine's Day*. Springfield, NJ: Enslow Publishers, 1990.

Freeman, Dorothy Rhodes. *St. Patrick's Day*. Springfield, NJ: Enslow Publishers, 1992.

Freeman, Dorothy Rhodes, and Dianne M. MacMillan. *Kwanzaa*. Springfield, NJ: Enslow Publishers, 1992.

Ghazi, Suhaib Hamil. *Ramadan*. New York: Holiday House, 1996.

Gore, Willma Willis. *Earth Day*. Springfield, NJ: Enslow Publishers, 1992.

——. *Mother's Day*. Springfield, NJ: Enslow Publishers, 1993.

Green, Robert. *Queen Victoria*. New York: Franklin Watts, 1998.

Herda, D. J. *Christmas*. New York: Franklin Watts, 1983.

Hoyt-Goldsmith, Diane. *Day of the Dead: A Mexican-American Celebration*. New York: Holiday House, 1994.

Johnson, Dolores. *The Children's Book of Kwanzaa*. New York: Aladdin Paperbacks, 1997.

Kaur-Singh, Kanwaljit. *Sikhism*. New York: Thomson Learning, 1995.

Kennedy, Pamela. *An Easter Celebration: Traditions and Customs from Around the World*. Nashville: Ideal Children's Books, 1990.

Kessel, Joyce K. *St. Patrick's Day*. Minneapolis: Carolrhoda Books, 1982.

Lasky, Kathryn. *Days of the Dead*. New York: Hyperion Books for Children, 1994.

Levy, Patricia. *Ireland*. New York: Marshall Cavendish, 1994.

Lowery, Linda. *Martin Luther King Day*. Minneapolis: Carolrhoda Books, 1987.

MacMillan, Dianne M. *Chinese New Year*. Springfield, NJ: Enslow Publishers, 1994.

——. *Diwali: Hindu Festival of Lights*. Springfield, NJ: Enslow Publishers, 1997.

——. *Easter*. Springfield, NJ: Enslow Publishers, 1993.

——. *Japanese Children's Day and the Obon Festival*. Springfield, NJ: Enslow Publishers, 1997.

——. *Jewish Holidays in the Fall*. Springfield, NJ: Enslow Publishers, 1993.

——. *Mardi Gras*. Springfield, NJ: Enslow Publishers, 1997.

——. *Mexican Independence Day and Cinco de Mayo*. Springfield, NJ: Enslow Publishers, 1997.

——. *Ramadan and Id al-Fitr*. Springfield, NJ: Enslow Publishers, 1994.

——. *Tet: Vietnamese New Year*. Springfield, NJ: Enslow Publishers, 1994.

Odor, Ruth Shannon. *Halloween Handbook*. Chicago: Children's Press, 1984.

Penner, Lucille Recht. *Celebration: The Story of American Holidays*. New York: Macmillan, 1993.

Resnick, Abraham. *The Holocaust*. San Diego: Lucent Books, 1991.

Rosen, Mike. *Spring Festivals*. New York: Bookwright Press, 1991.

Sandak, Cass R. *Halloween*. New York: Crestwood House, 1990.

——. *Patriotic Holidays*. New York: Crestwood House, 1990.

——. *Thanksgiving*. New York: Franklin Watts, 1980.

——. *Valentine's Day*. New York: Franklin Watts, 1980.

Spier, Arthur. *The Comprehensive Hebrew Calendar*. Nanuet, NY: Feldheim Publishers, 1986.

Strahinich, Helen. *The Holocaust: Understanding and Remembering*. Springfield, NJ: Enslow Publishing, 1996.

Walter, Mildred Pitts. *Kwanzaa: A Family Affair*. New York: Lothrop, Lee & Shepard Books, 1995.

Wangu, Madhu Bazaz. *Hinduism*. New York: Facts on File, 1991.

Winchester, Faith. *Muslim Holidays*. Mankato: Bridgestone Books, 1996.

Index

Picture Credits